BREAKING INTO PRINT

Breaking into print

BEING A COMPILATION OF PAPERS

WHEREIN

EACH OF A SELECT GROUP OF AUTHORS

TELLS

OF THE DIFFICULTIES OF AUTHORSHIP

HOW SUCH TRIALS ARE MET

TOGETHER WITH

BIOGRAPHICAL NOTES AND COMMENT
BY AN EDITOR OF THE COLOPHON

ELMER ADLER

Essay Index Reprint Series

 BOOKS FOR LIBRARIES PRESS
FREEPORT, NEW YORK

First Published 1937
Reprinted 1968

LIBRARY OF CONGRESS CATALOG CARD NUMBER:

68-55840

MANUFACTURED
BY
HALLMARK LITHOGRAPHERS, INC.
IN THE U.S.A.

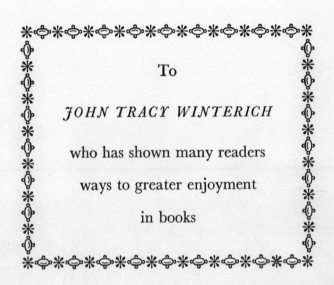

To

JOHN TRACY WINTERICH

who has shown many readers

ways to greater enjoyment

in books

FOREWORD

A book is born when it is published.

Kipling says in his autobiography, "Any fool, I knew to my sorrow, could write." Later he adds, "Any other fool could review." Between the writing and the reviewing comes that creative advent, the breaking into print.

Sometimes the experience may be simple and almost painless; sometimes it may be long-drawn-out and disheartening. The variations seem limited only by the number of participants. And now, in this book, twenty authors describe in a friendly, intimate, almost confessional manner, how they went through the experience of getting published. An unusually sympathetic audience inspired these revelations. Those who promptly gave support to The Colophon, when the quarterly was announced in 1929, revered the authors of the books they loved. The authors quickly sensed the feeling and quality of this group, and expressed themselves freely, in a manner almost "off the record." Thus during five years The Colophon gathered twenty of these confessions.

In order to tell the readers of this book how each of the authors works, a group of questions was prepared and mailed. And in the course of time, after some prodding here and there, all the answers arrived and now appear in the biographical notes. They vary not only in length but also in the methods they describe. One author explains that he puts nothing on paper until his thought is in a final state; he does not even revise the proof of the type form. Another begins with sketchy notes, which are supplemented and extended, rewritten and condensed; his number of changes is determined solely by the urgency of going to press. Because many of these explanations have so welcome an informality they are presented here as they were written. Occasionally, however, as the reader will observe, the editor added a few words. Two authors represented in this book have died, but their literary executors and friends have supplied the desired information. Whenever practical, the author's explanation is accompanied by the reproduction of a portion of manuscript. Thus the reader can see the writer's way of working.

In his report on the first years of The Colophon*, John T. Winterich tells how the series of articles on Breaking Into Print originated and grew, even though an occasional author departed from the original theme and discussed some other phase of writing. At times the editors themselves suggested a different theme, as when we wrote to Mrs. Wharton for confirmation of a story that Lincoln Kirstein brought back from Paris. For the most part, however, these papers are confined to the trial of getting started—an experience every writer must have before he will arrive anywhere.

Successful writers are bitterly aware of the pitfalls that await anyone who attempts to reach the goal of authorship. Those gathered here have reached firm ground, and well may pause, turn, and offer to share their experience with others who have done no more than dream of breaking into print.

E. A.

New York, April, 1937

* INDEX, The Colophon, New York, 1935

Table of Contents

SHERWOOD ANDERSON *On Being Published,* 3
facsimile of manuscript page, facing page 6

ROBERT BENCHLEY *Why Does Nobody Collect Me?,* 9
facsimile of manuscript page, facing page 14

STEPHEN VINCENT BENÉT *The Sixth Man,* 19

PEARL BUCK *The Writing of* East Wind: West Wind, 29

JAMES BRANCH CABELL *Recipes for Writers,* 35
facsimile of manuscript page, facing page 39

CHARLES WADDELL CHESNUTT
Post-Bellum-Pre-Harlem, 47
facsimile of manuscript page, facing page 54

A. E. COPPARD *On First Getting into Print,* 57
facsimile of manuscript page, facing page 60

THEODORE DREISER
The Early Adventures of Sister Carrie, 67

JOSEPH HERGESHEIMER *Biography and Bibliographies,* 73
facsimile of manuscript page, facing page 76

ROBINSON JEFFERS *First Book,* 85
facsimile of manuscript page, facing page 87

MACKINLAY KANTOR *My Memoirs of the Civil War,* 93
facsimile of manuscript page, facing page 102

[ix]

ROCKWELL KENT *Alias Kent, by Hogarth, Jr.,* 105
facsimile of manuscript page, facing page 106

SINCLAIR LEWIS *Breaking into Print,* 117
facsimile of manuscript page, facing page 119

WILLIAM McFEE *Getting into Print,* 125
facsimile of manuscript page, facing page 134

H. L. MENCKEN *On Breaking into Type,* 139
facsimile of manuscript page, facing page 142

CHRISTOPHER MORLEY *The Eighth Sin,* 147

EDWIN ARLINGTON ROBINSON *The First Seven Years,* 161
facsimile of manuscript page, facing page 167

CARL VAN VECHTEN *Notes for an Autobiography,* 171

HUGH WALPOLE *My First Published Book,* 179
facsimile of manuscript page, facing page 182

EDITH WHARTON *The Writing of* Ethan Frome, 187
facsimile of manuscript page, facing page 190

BREAKING INTO PRINT

SHERWOOD ANDERSON

Born Camden, Ohio, September 13, 1876.
Educated in public schools. Spanish-American War veteran. Worked as timekeeper, factory manager, advertising copy writer, editor and publisher of Democratic and Republican newspapers simultaneously. Married. Author *Windy McPherson's Son* (1916), *Winesburg, Ohio* (1919), *A Story Teller's Story* (1924), *Dark Laughter* (1925). Home: Troutdale, Virginia.

ON BEING PUBLISHED appeared in Part One of The Colophon; February, 1930.

Ripshin Farm
Troutdale, Va.
December 27, 1936

Dear Elmer:

As I am not much of a desk man I write anywhere and everywhere, usually on cheap yellow tablets that can be got in any small stationery store. Sometimes I write out a complete story thus, but do not look at it afterwards when I get to the typewriter.

I have always had rather a hard time making a living by my writing. For ten or fifteen years, after I began writing, I had to live by writing advertisements. I was engaged by a large advertising agency and have written many of my stories surrounded by

[3]

the hub-bub of such a place. I had to travel a good deal and wrote often in the day coach of some train or in a railroad station. It may be that all this did teach me concentration.

I am too impatient about corrections, spelling and punctuation. I get excited when I work and pound the typewriter unmercifully. The damn machine is always out of order.

And there is something else. There are too many stories in my head. When I have written out a story, the first draft, I want to forget it, get on to another. I keep thinking I can do better with the next one. Often my wife digs up a story of mine from a pile of discarded manuscript. "What's the matter with this story?" she asks.

"Let me see it." I read. "Why, it is pretty good. Why don't you try to sell it?" Fortunately both my wife and my mother-in-law seem to love digging up mistakes in spelling, punctuation, etc. I can hear them in the next room laughing at me. When they get through with it they have it typed for me.

They have everything to do with proofs from printers, occasionally coming to consult me. . . I must say sometimes with a slightly patronizing air. "What word did you think you were trying to write in here?" they say.

Copy, yes. There are tons of it about. My wife will take charge of that.

Sherwood

Sherwood Anderson

THERE MUST have been a few other things. I dare say I always scribble. I was a copy man in an advertising agency in Chicago.

One day Mr. Cyrus Curtis came in. He had been attracted to something I wrote. He wanted to see the man who wrote it. It must have been something about business, I can't remember.

However, his being attracted to it helped me. Mr. Curtis was already a big man in that advertising world. I got a raise out of that.

In some of my books I have told about a certain factory I later owned in Ohio. The tale is in *A Story Teller's Story*. The truth is the factory was about ready to go to pieces. I was doing too much writing. I didn't attend to business, didn't want to. Things were ready for a break.

The break, when it came, went deep. All the life I had built up was ruined. I had been trying to be a "regular fellow." I belonged to clubs, went about with salesmen, business men, etc.

I was leading a double life. I went home to my house and into a room upstairs. Often I didn't come down to dinner. I wrote all night. I was strong. My body stood it all right.

About my nerves I don't know. I wrote hundreds of words in that room and threw the sheets away. My wife must have thought me crazy.

[5]

I am sure I did not have any great passion to be a writer. I haven't now.

I did seek something.

Perhaps I felt my own life, rather at the core, during that time.

I remember the scene from the window of that room. There were two gardens I could see into. One man went in for flowers, the other for vegetables. I couldn't decide which was the most beautiful.

Right now it seems to me I can see every flower, every vegetable, in those two gardens. I can see the gardens at the various stages of the seasons. I must have been writing like that madly, in that room for at least two years.

Both the gardeners, who were my neighbors, were orderly men. I had a passion for order in myself. I wanted some sort of rhythm, a swing to life—my life and other lives.

I never got it in fact.

I have approached it sometimes, on the printed page.

*   *   *

As for being published the first time. It was a story called "The Rabbit Pen" and was published in *Harper's*. I am pretty sure it was not a very fine story. I have never read it since. I never included it in any book of stories, never wanted to.

Why? I don't know why.

*   *   *

Being published made no great impression. At that time I was in a hospital at Cleveland.

Well, I had walked away from my factory, from that room, that town, all my life there. Perhaps my brain had cracked a little. I was an uneducated man. Many people had told me I could not write.

[6]

My notions seemed immoral to all the people I knew. I knew no artists.

There had been this intense struggle, within myself. Perhaps if I had stayed there in that place and had attended to business I would have got rich.

I did not want that either nor did I want specially to be published. What of all that? There was already too much rot published.

I was in a hospital to be examined for mental disorder. They did examine me there. I had left that factory and that town and had wandered about the country for days.

I was trying to find some order, some sense, in my own life and in other lives. They picked me up and took me to the hospital.

They were very kind to me there. Everyone was very kind. I must have written that story in that room looking into the gardens. I don't remember writing it. I must have sent it to that magazine.

Someone brought the letter, accepting the story, or the magazine with it in, to my bed in the hospital.

Perhaps they felt it a proof of my mental unsoundness that I was not elated. I wasn't. As a matter of fact it would be better for the art of prose writing if all stories were published unsigned.

I knew I had not got at what I wanted a little to get at in that story.

It was published. Well, the thing I was after, am still after, was just as far away as it had been before.

ROBERT C. BENCHLEY

Born in Worcester, Massachusetts, September 15, 1889.
A.B., Harvard, 1912. Secretary to Aircraft Board, Washington, D. C., 1917-1918. Worked as advertising man, industrial personnel director, Sunday supplement and magazine editor, dramatic critic with *Life* and *The New Yorker*, actor in musical shows and short talking films. Married. Author of *Of All Things* (1921), *Love Conquers All* (1922), *The Treasurer's Report* (1930), *My Ten Years in a Quandary* (1936). Home: Scarsdale, New York.

WHY DOES NOBODY COLLECT ME? appeared in Part Eighteen of The Colophon, with special designs by William Steig; September, 1934.

44 West 44th St.
New York City
February 16, 1937

Dear Adler:

I hope that I am not too late to contribute the following priceless items to your Natural History of Belles Lettres:

I can not write more than three or four lines of longhand without fainting. Even if I could, I wouldn't be able to compose on anything but a typewriter, probably a bad habit from newspaper days. I don't make notes in advance, because I don't know in advance what the piece is to be about. I am lucky if I know what the next paragraph is going to be about.

My copy goes right to the printers as I write it, and, if I do say so, they consider it very "clean." This is due to my inability to go on with a page of copy if it has more than well, maybe three penciled corrections on it. This mania for clean copy, or rather phobia against unclean copy, is one of the strange quirks in an otherwise sloppy nature. It even goes so far as to make it almost impossible for me to write on a typewriter which has a spotty ribbon or (and here is where I get into the temperamental class) type which is much larger or less black than this.

I like to have a page of copy look as much like a galley-proof as possible, and am not very popular with copy-readers for my little whim of single-spacing such small type, because, although I may not want to pencil in corrections, they do. For this purpose I leave a very wide margin, so that changes may be indicated there as on a galley-proof, instead of penciling them in over the words. (As an example of my nervousness over margins, the slip in the alignment in this paragraph is driving me crazy, and I would do the whole thing over, except that it is a good point in this rather unimportant exposition.)

In all this, you will understand that I prepare no copy at all for my books, as they are all made up of reprints of articles published elsewhere and go to Harper's as clippings. The only copy that I prepare is for the newspaper and magazine printers. I get one set of proofs for the magazine stuff, but none on the newspaper material. From Harper's I get a set of galleys, which I am unable to read through, being so sick of the stuff already. I answer the queries, and that's all. As a result, in my last book, there was a whole line misplaced, giving the paragraph no sense at all. I hadn't

A·C·D·E·F·G·H·I·J·K·L·M·R·B·N·O·P·Q·S·T·U·V·W·X·Y·Z

caught it in the proof, because I hadn't read it, and evidently the proof-reader at Harper's didn't notice the difference.

The only changes I make after the stuff is in type are cuts. I used to be an editor myself. In fact, once the copy is out of my hands, I don't care if I never see it again. And I usually don't.

I certainly took you at your word and gave you information galore.

Sincerely,

Robert Benchley

P.S. There must be some better way of governing that right-hand margin. Just look at it!

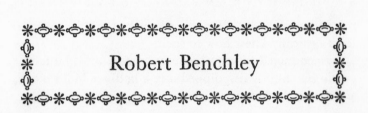

Robert Benchley

SOME MONTHS AGO, while going through an old box of books looking for a pressed nasturtium, I came across a thin volume which, even to my dreamer's instinct, seemed worth holding out, if only for purposes of prestige.

It was a first edition of Ernest Hemingway's *In Our Time*, the edition brought out in Paris by the Three Mountains Press in 1924, while Hemingway was just "Old Ernie" who lived over the saw-mill in the rue Notre Dames des Champs. I knew that it must be worth saving, because it said in the front that the edition consisted of one hundred and seventy copies, of which mine was Number Thirty-nine. That usually means something.

It so happened that, a few weeks later, "Old Ernie" himself was using my room in New York as a hide-out from literary columnists and reporters during one of his stop-over visits between Africa and Key West. On such all-too-rare occasions he lends an air of virility to my dainty apartment which I miss sorely after he has gone and the furniture has been repaired.

More to interrupt his lion-hunting story than anything else, I brought out my copy of *In Our Time* and suggested that, in memory of happy days around the Anise Deloso bowl at the Closerie des Lilas, it might be the handsome thing for him to inscribe a few pally sentiments on the fly-leaf. Not, as I took pains to explain to him, that I was a

particular admirer of his work, so much as that I wanted to
see if he really knew how to spell.

Encouraged by my obviously friendly tone, he took a
pen in his chubby fist, dipped it in a bottle of bull's blood,
and wrote the following:

> *To Robert ("Garbage Bird") Benchley,*
> *hoping that he won't wait for prices*
> *to reach the peak——*
> > *from his friend,*
> > *Ernest ("—— ——") Hemingway*

The "Garbage Bird" reference in connection with me
was a familiarity he had taken in the past to describe my
appearance in the early morning light of Montparnasse on
certain occasions. The epithet applied to himself, which
was unprintable except in *Ulysses*, was written deliberately
to make it impossible for me to cash in on the book.

Then, crazed with success at defacing *In Our Time*, he
took my first edition of *A Farewell to Arms* and filled in each
blank in the text where Scribner's had blushed and put a
dash instead of the original word. I think that he supplied
the original word in every case. In fact, I am sure of it.

On the fly-leaf of this he wrote:

> *To R. (G). B. from E.(–). H.*
> *Corrected edition. Filled-in blanks.*
> *Very valuable. Sell quick.*

Now, oddly enough, I had never considered selling
either book. I had known, in a general way, that a first
edition of the Gutenberg Bible would be worth money, and
that, if one could lay hands on an autographed copy of
Canterbury Tales, it would be a good idea to tuck it away,
but that a first edition of one of Ernie's books could be the
object of even Rabelaisian jesting as to its commercial value
surprised and, in a vague sort of way, depressed me. Why

NEW GRIST

"King Richard II" may have been unfamiliar Shakespeare before its presentation last week at the St. James, but before the season is over, it should rank with "Hamlet" in any estimate of the Bard's 1937 showing on Broadway. Not that it is as good a play as "Hamlet", although it has many speeches which may sound lovlier because they are fresher to our ears, but Maurice Evans gives it such high distinction that it might very well come in a winner---and paying 100 to 1, which is the more remarkable.

Mr. Evans plays the weakling king with none of the ham usually associated with successful Shakespearean performances, but loses none of the force which hamminess ~~supplies~~ supplies. He has already Romeo, the Dauphin of France and Napoleon to his credit in this country, and his Richard tops them all; in fact, it comes pretty close to topping the season. And, when you consider how unimpressive the mens' clothes were in those days, his feat becomes doubly surprising. It ~~is~~ is easy enough to cut a figure as Hamlet in black tights and a gold chain , but when you have to walk across the stage trailing a heavy dressing gown which looks too large for you, and wearing a hat which even a woman of today would shy away from, the art of looking like a king, even a weak one, becomes prodigious.

In making "Richard II" into a thrilling play, Mr. Evans is aided by such good Shakespeareans as Ian Kieth, Augustin ~~Smith~~ Duncan, Charles Dalton and Whitford Kane (the last must hardly know the difference between his role of gardener and the grave-digger in "Hamlet", so fast they "tread upon another's heel") and Eddie Dowling and Robinson Smith have given

are not *my* works matters for competitive bidding in the open market?

I am older than Hemingway, and have written more books than he has. And yet it is as much as my publishers and I can do to get people to pay even the list-price for my books, to say nothing of a supplementary sum for rare copies. One of my works, *Love Conquers All*, is even out of print, and yet nobody shows any interest in my extra copy. I have even found autographed copies of my books in secondhand book shops, along with *My Life and Times* by Buffalo Bill. Doesn't *any*body care?

What is there about me and my work that repels collectors? I am handsome, in an unusual sort of way, and speak French fluently, even interspersing some of my writings with French phrases. True, some of my copy, as it goes to the printer, is not strictly orthodox in spelling and punctuation, but the proofreaders have always been very nice about it, and, by the time my books are out, there is nothing offensive to the eye about them. And yet I have been told by hospital authorities that more copies of my works are left behind by departing patients than those of any other author. It does seem as if people might at least take my books home with them.

If it is rarity which counts in the value of a book, I have dozens of very rare Benchley items in my room which I know can not be duplicated. For the benefit of collectors, I will list them, leaving the price more or less up to the would-be purchaser. All that I ask is that I don't actually lose money on the sale.

There is a copy of my first book, *Of All Things*, issued by Henry Holt in 1922. (Mr. Lincoln MacVeagh, who engineered the deal, is now Ambassador to Greece, which ought to count for something.) It is a first edition, an author's copy, in fact, and has a genuine tumbler-ring on the cover. I have no doubt that it is actually the first volume of mine ever to be issued, and, as *Of All Things* has gradually gone into twelve editions since, it ought to be very valuable. Page 29 is dog-eared.

Love Conquers All (Holt–1923) is, as I have said, now out of print, which makes my extra copy almost unique. I doubt very much if any one else has an *extra* copy of *Love Conquers All*. It is a third edition, which may detract a little from its market value, but this is compensated for by the fact that it belonged originally to Dorothy Parker, who left it at my house five or six years ago and has never felt the need for picking it up. So, you see, it is really a Dorothy Parker item, too.

Pluck and Luck (Holt–1924) was brought out later in a dollar edition for drugstore sale, and I have three of those in a fair state of preservation. One of them is a very interesting find for collectors, as I had started to inscribe it to Donald Ogden Stewart and then realized that I had spelled the name "Stuart," necessitating the abandonment of the whole venture. It is practically certain that there is not another dollar edition of *Pluck and Luck* with Donald Ogden Stewart's name spelled "Stuart" on the fly-leaf. Would a dollar and a quarter be too much to ask, do you think?

Faulty inscriptions account for most of the extra copies of *The Early Work* (Holt–1926) that I have, lying about. It was during that period, and that of my next book, *Twenty Thousand Leagues Under the Sea, or David Copperfield* (Holt–1928) that I went through a phase of trying to write humorous remarks on the fly-leaves of gift-copies. Those copies in which the remarks did not turn out to be so humorous as I had planned had to be put aside. I have eighteen or twenty of these discarded copies, each with an inscription which is either unfunny or misspelled.

During what I call "my transitional period," when I changed from Henry Holt to Harper's and began putting on weight, I was moody and fretful, and so did not feel like trying to make wisecracks in my inscriptions. The recipient of a book was lucky if I even took the trouble to write his name in it. He was lucky, indeed, if he could read *my* name, for it was then that I was bullied into autographing copies at book-shop teas (this was my transitional period, you must remember, and I was not myself), and my handwriting deteriorated into a mere series of wavy lines, like static.

For this reason, I have not so many curious copies of *The Treasurer's Report* and *No Poems* hanging about. I have, however, a dummy of *The Treasurer's Report* with each page blank, and many of my friends insist that it should be worth much more than the final product. I don't know just how dummy-copies rate as collectors' items, but I will be very glad to copy the entire text into it longhand for fifty dollars. Thirty-five dollars, then.

And now I come to what I consider the choicest item of them all—one which would shape up rather impressively in a glass case a hundred years from now. It is a complete set of corrected galleys for my next book (to be called, I am afraid, *From Bed to Worse*) which I had cut up for rearrangement before I realized that I was cutting up the wrong set of proofs—the one that the printer wants back. I haven't broken the news to the printer at Harper's, and I may never get up the courage to do so (printers get so cross), in which case the book will never come out at all. Would that be a valuable piece of property or not—a set of hand-corrected galleys for a Benchley item which never was published? And all cut up into little sections, too! A veritable treasure, I would call it, although possibly the words might come better from somebody else.

But, until the collecting public comes to its senses, I seem to be saddled, not only with a set of mutilated galleys, but about twenty-five rare copies of my earlier works, each unique in its way. Possibly Hemingway would like them in return for the two books of his own that he has gone to so much trouble to render unsaleable for me.

STEPHEN VINCENT BENÉT

Born Bethlehem, Pennsylvania, July 22, 1898.
B.A., Yale, 1919, M.A., 1920. Married. John Simon Guggenheim Fellowship in 1926 and 1927. Author: *The Beginning of Wisdom* (1921), *John Brown's Body* (1928), *Ballads and Poems* (1921). Home: New York.

THE SIXTH MAN appeared in Part Fifteen of The Colophon; October, 1933.

The questions asked of Mr. Benét were:

(1) Do you use a typewriter?
(2) Is your copy retyped by someone else?
(3) Do you correct more than one proof?
(4) Do you make many changes?
(5) Have you a characteristic bit of copy for reproducing?

and his answers:

220 East 69th St.
New York

(1) I write in longhand.

(2) I type it myself.

(3) On a book, I get the usual galley and page proofs. That's enough.

(4) Not many. It depends.

(5) Most of mine—in pencil on manila second-sheets—would not reproduce well.

Sincerely

S. V. B.

Stephen Vincent Benét

ANY small boy, with elders and betters whom he admires, is going to try his own hand at imitating their activities. The admiration, of course, is necessary. But I did admire mine. On the other hand, I knew when I was first put into spectacles—around eight I think it was—that I probably never would be an army officer like my father. Spectacles were spectacles and the military life was the military life.

Of course, there are always exceptions, and, like others, I have led heroic charges against indefinite but numerous enemies and died with a modest but satisfied smile on my stern lips while the bearded veterans of my Guard sobbed about me like little children. But, even then, the spectacles were rather in the way.

However, there were other activities and other things to imitate. I can't remember my father without hearing his voice, quoting what he liked or what had become part of his mind—quoting, sometimes, with an ironic twist not intended by the author. "Shed no tear, oh, shed no tear!" "No more, O nevermore Will bloom the thunder-blasted tree Or the striken eagle soar." "Now listen to this hoary man Who leans upon his oar." "In Tilbury Town did old King Cole." He was, perhaps, a singular army officer. I think few men in the Army of his time combined as exact a knowledge of the Byzantine emperors with as deep an appreciation of the works of James B. Elmore. He was also able to command a camp of ten thousand men and enjoy that too. But that was in later days. I am trying to remember the first ones, now.

And, from the first days I knew him until his death, his influence upon me was very great. He could not stand the mediocre or the pompous in letters—but to the best and the very worst he gave a profound and discriminating affection. He had one of the finest collections of really bad verse —the true, inimitable yelp of a trodden language—that ever graced a set of library shelves. Not that his taste stopped there. He was apt to find the genuine before most people found it and he would have been the fortune of a publisher. I don't know where he picked up Wells' *Conversations With An Uncle* or Stephen Crane's *Black Riders* or the early peoms of Francis Thompson or *Almayer's Folly* or some of the first magazine-pieces of Edwin Arlington Robinson. But he did and told us about them before they were known.

He wasn't a collector and cared nothing about editions. He looked for the living thing and, though he had definite dislikes, his mind never hardened into a rigid pattern. His scrapbooks were burned in a family fire. I could have spared a good deal else that went before I spared them, because they gave a little of the history of his taste and judgment. There were a good many poems in those three scrapbooks and not one commonplace one, though there were large names and smaller. For one thing, his standards, though catholic, had foundation and he was both a severe and a comprehending critic of the actual technique of verse. He knew how the thing should be done, though he did not practise it, except for impromptu family-occasions and *bouts-rimes*. And when I say that he knew how the thing should be done, I am not paying his memory an empty compliment. I mean precisely that. When his children came to write, he did not criticize their work from the point of view of an indiscriminate affection, and there was not the slightest trace of the amateur in any of his judg-

ments. You could agree with them or disagree with them—
and both my brother and myself have often done the latter.
But we knew they were professional, even when we dis-
agreed.

So I remember that first—the big house with the big
porch and all California outside and my father's voice,
coming out of the warm evening, as he sat in a cane chair
and talked about people and books. Sometimes he and my
mother would argue one point or another—she was and is
a lady of spirit and her own mind. She had the story-teller's
gift and the wish, now and then, to put it down on paper,
but she was too busy, living. The stars came out, big in the
sky, and I listened to them both, and to other voices, until
I got too sleepy to listen. It was twenty-five years ago and
that always sounds a very long time, in books. It may all be
existing still, the porch and the faces and the talk, on some
light-ray going away from the earth. If it does, it is no
stranger to think of, for me, than that it was twenty-five
years ago.

My brother and sister came home from college, that
summer, and both were writing. It didn't seem odd to me
that they should do so, it didn't seem odd that they should
take a nine-year-old boy into their confidence and let him
see what they had written and give his own views. Of
course, the boy was flattered, but it didn't seem odd. It was
as natural to write verse and like writing verse and struggle
fiendishly to get it the way one wanted as it was to ride
horses or go on picnics or command a battalion. Everybody
agreed that there was no money to be made in writing it,
but then there was no money to be made in the Army, in
the sense of fortune. The two things—money and reward—
were entirely disparate and one worked for something else.

I am stating so much because, usually, in books about
writers, the writer has to struggle rather animatedly against
a hostile home environment. The villagers throw stones at
him, Brother Ben comes back from butchering the pigs just

[23]

in time to light the oast-house fire with his love-lyrics and
the rest of the clan is always trying to force him into
the leather-business. He is pretty misunderstood and
chivied, in fact, throughout the first six chapters, and, even
if he has a pet lark, it usually dies. There is one person, to
be sure, who does appreciate him, often a lady piano-
teacher, but as everybody in town calls her "that queer
Miss Miggs," she really isn't much help. Finally, when
things become critical and the assembled family-circle
wrenches his secret from him—the secret he has tried so
hard to conceal from their coarse, appraising eyes—he is
driven out into the snow with his shawl-wrapped bundle of
manuscript in the crook of his arm.

It is all extremely exciting and unsympathetic and
must be a lot of fun for everyone concerned. But I cannot
write of it from personal experience. There is always a
sufficient amount of opposition, misconstruction and hostility in life for any writer. But I got none of it from my
family, then or later. They never suggested that I write or
stop writing, or that I was a peculiar person to be doing
either. They listened, with patience, to verse, prose and
extempore plays. They did not appear to be awestruck over
my inimitable gifts nor did they laugh at my folly. They
treated me as an adult, with adult responsibilities. And,
somehow, I got from their attitude, among others, one very
important thing—that it was the work which mattered,
not the name or the age or the circumstances.

That was one thing. There were a great many others.
There were the books and in the books the poetry that had
been written. And there was my brother, in the study with
the red and yellow grass matting on the floor, writing it.
I could hear him walking up and down; now and then he
would say "Oh, God!" He covered yellow paper with
crossed-out lines and crumpled up the sheets in the waste-
basket—then, eventually, the typewriter would begin. It
was an old Smith Premier with separate keys for capitals

A·C·D·E·F·G·H·I·J·K·L·M·S·V·B·N·O·P·Q·R·T·U·W·X·Y·Z

and lower case—it looked, somehow, formidable and full of
teeth. Afterwards, he would sometimes read it aloud to
some of us or all of us. If I came in, when he had just finished, he might read it to me. A poet with a new poem will
read it to a child, a wall or a tree, if necessary.

I never had any delusion that it was easy to write
poetry—I never had any delusion that it was not an intense
and shaking delight, at the best, when the current ran. I
admired my brother very much, and had reason. I remember lying out on the side of a long slope with the dry brown
grass of summer higher than my head and hearing him
read me a poem he had just finished, "The Halcyon Birds."
It was, and is, a beautiful poem. I knew good poems, in
books. But this wasn't in a book, yet; it had been written in
the last week, in the study with the straw matting, by the
brother who drew and colored figures for my toy theatre
and kicked a football with me and was, in all ways, what
an elder brother can be to a younger one. Before this week,
it had not existed at all.

So, even when I went to school and was taught how to
parse *Snow-Bound* with diagrams, I knew poetry was not a
dead thing or an alien thing or a dry game of words. I
knew there were rules and that you could break the rules
but that you must never break them unintentionally. I
knew it was always written by the living, even though the
date-line said that the man was dead.

So there wasn't any writing in secret or hiding verses
under a plank in the barn. I wanted to write and I wanted
to see it in print—print had an authenticity that even the
neatest typewriting lacked. And a poem called "The Re-
gret of Dives" is the high-water mark of my juvenile career.
I was under the impression that *Dives* rhymed with *hives*,
but, fortunately, the name only occurred in the title, and
the St. Nicholas League awarded me a special cash-prize
of three dollars. It was a good deal of money to spend on a
train coming back from California to the East and it must

have satisfied a primal urge, for I didn't do much writing for the next couple of years.

We had moved to Georgia, by then, and my brother had gone away, to work in New York, marry, become assistant editor of the *Century Magazine* and publish two books. But I still saw a great deal of him, and when I was sixteen and, abruptly, the wish and desire to write came back, I knew very definitely that that was what I wanted to do. I wrote a couple of poems that fall and suddenly the lines were, to me, lifelike. There is nothing like the first taste of that. It is a gigantic pleasure; it is also, in some respects, a curiously selfless one. All the hot-and-cold vanity of the author is in it, of course, and yet, when that is over, now and then, at brief moments, the lines seem to walk by themselves, to have their own entity. And that is enough, that is all that can be asked or demanded, ever, at any time.

Of course they were terrible poems but I was fortunate enough not to know it. There is a time when words like "golden," "glorious," "splendid" seem neither inexact nor well-known but golden, glorious, splendid new-minted discoveries, shining with their own light. There is a time when one feels perfectly competent to write the best poem ever written about Helen of Troy and plan a five-act Elizabethan tragedy that will greatly improve on Hamlet, at least in the number of casualties. My own Renaissance tragedy had only one act and four characters—a Duke, his Duchess, her lover Amaldo and an off-stage tiger in a cage —but it made up for it in action. The Duke trapped Amaldo into the cage, the Duchess pushed in the Duke and then, after soliloquy, took the most obvious way to rejoin both Duke and lover. In the end, the curtain fell upon a completely empty stage—and a full tiger. I need hardly add that it was written in blank verse.

Meanwhile, I had been reading Masefield's *Tragedy of Pompey* and Ferrero's *History of Rome*. I don't know which of the two led me to the other. But I soaked in them both, that

winter and the next spring, and in the work of a number of
other poets. So it is hardly remarkable that nearly everything I wrote wavered between one imitation and another.
But I had a very good time. I wrote about knights, gods,
pirates, the Nephilim, death, the sea and love. I had never
seen or experienced any of them, except the sea, but that
did not seem to hamper me. It was not modesty that kept
me from meditating another epic on the Fall of Man, but
actual lack of time.

For, around June of 1915, two things happened to me.
I had two longish poems actually accepted by adult magazines and I flunked thirteen of my entrance examinations
to Yale College. My father imported a tutor and we stayed
in Georgia that summer, instead of going to the mountains.
I shall always feel very grateful to Donald Bridgman for
two things—he tutored me so efficiently that I was able to
enter Yale that fall and he did not work me on Sundays. So
every Sunday, during that Summer, I wrote a poem.

I think the six poems that make up *Five Men and Pompey* were written on successive Sundays, though I am no
longer sure. But it was a good summer. There was the
bright heat of July and August in the air, and the red dust
on the clay tennis-court, and the thunderstorm that came
every evening to cool things off. There was Boyle's Law
and the date of the Reform Bill and the ablative absolute
and writing till my feet felt cold. There was my brother's
letter saying that the *Century* had accepted "The Hemp"
and John Wolcott Adams was to illustrate it and my father's
voice saying the song in "Lucullus Dines—" was really
rather pretty but the blank verse showed the influence of
Browning. It was a good time, it was also a culmination,
though I did not know that. I was not to come back to
Georgia again, except for vacations. And, after that, I began to be someone else.

My brother took the Pompey poems and arranged
for their publication with the Four Seas Company of

Boston. I should be able to remember exactly when that happened, but I don't, although I was unutterably pleased. It was to be a surprise but, somehow or other, I got to know about it before the book actually came out. I don't even remember correcting proof—perhaps my brother did that. But I do remember one thing—the book was to have a cover-design by Elihu Vedder. I had seen his illustrations for the Rubáiyát and expected something enormous. I wouldn't have cared, particularly, if the book had been printed on towel-paper as long as it was actually published. But a cover-design by a well-known artist is a cover-design by a well-known artist. I wondered which particular scene he would choose.

The author's copies of the book reached me in December, all alike, all small, definite, firm, unused. There was nothing more to do about it; it existed. I read it through immediately with mingled pleasure and hopelessness and thought it was magnificent and that I would do better next time. I had planned and thought about another book of the same size and sort dealing with the English Civil War, but it never got done. It couldn't get done, because, in the meantime, I started to grow up, and, in the process, something disappeared that, once lost, is lost. For this reason I can still look at the book, though the work in it has no value whatsoever and I cannot remember the author as well as I should.

I have been asked questions about the number of copies originally printed of *Five Men and Pompey* and I can only say that I do not know. I think there were three hundred—there may have been more, but, if so, I cannot imagine why. The first issue was bound in purple paper, over boards —it was quite a bright purple to start with but it has faded a good deal. In the middle of the cover is a design by Elihu Vedder—a carefully drawn Roman pot, about as big as a thumb-nail.

PEARL BUCK

Born Hillsboro, West Virginia, June 26, 1892.
Educated at home and in private boarding school at
Shanghai. A.B., Randolph-Macon Women's College, 1914.
M.A., Cornell, 1926. Missionary in China. Married. Au-
thor *East Wind: West Wind* (1929), *The Good Earth* (1932),
Sons (1932). Home: Perkasie, Bucks County, Pennsylvania,
and New York.

THE WRITING OF EAST WIND: WEST WIND
appeared in Part Twelve of The Colophon; December,
1932.

45 Prospect Place
New York
December 22, 1936

My dear Mr. Adler:

*I shall answer your questions about my writing as
briefly as possible, for your sake as well as mine.*

*I write in longhand now that I have someone to do my
typing. My first books I wrote directly on the typewriter and copied
them myself. Now I have someone else do this work for me in order
to save time and strength.*

*It would be quite impossible for me to dictate. In fact,
I can never work with anyone else in the room at all.*

No, I do not receive more than one proof. In fact, sometimes I do not look at any proof whatever. I make no change in my
copy after it is in type. In fact, I make very few changes anyway
because I have my stories very well thought out before I begin to
write at all. Once I begin to write, I write with considerable speed
and in the final form.

Sincerely yours,

Pearl S. Buck

Pearl Buck

W HEN I began to write *East Wind: West Wind* it was certainly not with any idea in my mind that later it might be put between the covers of a book. I wrote it in mid-Pacific, in the writing room or in odd corners of the lounge of an Empress liner. I was quite shut off from the world, for there is no more delightful privacy than the isolation of an English steamship, where each passenger fears equally speaking to or being spoken to by another, lest in such an act a fatal social mistake be made.

In this privacy the slender tale wove itself out, my first attempt to write anything longer than a little sketch. At its conclusion at the end of about fifty pages, I put it away and did nothing more with it until some months later when a valued friend asked with urgency why I had nothing written to show him. Ashamed of my delinquency, for he was ever urging me to write, I brought forth my story, written with the utmost illegibility upon ship's note paper.

After he had deciphered it, with pains, I am sure, although he was too kind to say so, he persevered until he had made me promise to type it and then I sent it to *Asia Magazine*. It was accepted and appeared as *A Chinese Woman Speaks*.

After its publication a well known New York publishing house wrote to me—I had then returned to China —asking me to enlarge the story into a full length novel and offering to publish it. Meantime I had written another story, in the nature of a sequel. I examined the first story again with some interest, naturally, but I decided that to enlarge it was to put too heavy a burden upon its frail structure. It was necessarily a delicate, limited tale, because I had unconsciously chosen in the first place that very limited point of view, a young girl's mind.

I wrote the publishers, therefore, that I could not with honesty enlarge the original story, but I offered the two stories together. This arrangement they refused.

The manuscript lay then for a year or two in a drawer, and I forgot it until one day a man said to me of it, "Why do you not put that story of yours into a book?"

I remembered it again, and I fetched it from its drawer, read it, and decided its chances were so slight that I could not trouble to retype it. Nevertheless, I decided I would send it to some literary agency and if a publisher could be found it would be well, and if not, then nothing was lost. I chose at random the names of three such agencies out of a handbook for writers I happened to have had given me. Two of the agencies replied saying they preferred to handle nothing from China, since editors and publishers were not interested at all in such material. The third agency wrote me that they would be glad to handle material dealing with China. I sent the manuscripts to them and it was accepted. I forgot it again in the series of exciting events in China. Mr. David Lloyd, my agent, will have me believe that its fortunes until it found a publisher were exciting to him. It seems to have been well read before publication, as it was on offer, Mr. Lloyd says, from one October till the next September through a period of forty-seven weeks. "Despite a prejudice," if one may quote one's agent—

"Despite a prejudice among those who publish books and sell them, we put our best Chinese foot forward about your manuscript from the start. The original selling memorandum—(a direct yet delicate portrayal of the new and the old in China)—still seems to fit aptly, and foretell the spirit

of its successors. For its readers, we chose successively publishers we knew were accessible to its flavor and authentic
substance, and—always up to a certain point—they re-
sponded to these temptations—editors of established lists,
publishers later in the field but not behind in a reputation.
It was the sort of manuscript such men are reluctant to
decline, a mental state often mistaken by inexperienced
writers for an editorial affectation. In one office everyone
would agree that the book was delightful, in another, one
convinced champion would fight for it as a thing of beauty,
in a third, five or six excited judges could compose the different bases of their interest only in respect to that well-
known prejudice—(it was believed in, only three short
years ago)—against Chinese books. In the Paget agency
itself we had to save our face as business men and women
by conferring on the question whether to go on offering a
book by Pearl S. Buck! We went on. In the forty-seventh
week, on the seventh day of the month, to borrow the ac-
cent of Noah in his Ark, the book found its imprint. Richard
Walsh and his associates, perhaps not without some prayer
and fasting of their own, decided to plump for it."

We made in that year, however, a hurried business
trip to America, and while we were there a letter was for-
warded to me from China, whither it had been sent by my
agent, saying that The John Day Company had made an
acceptable offer for the book and would I cable concerning
certain matters. At the instant of receiving this letter I happened to be but a few hours from New York; I had so
completely forgotten the whole matter that I had neglected
to tell the agency of my change of continents.

When I could, therefore, I went to New York and to
the John Day offices, and found that the title I had given
the manuscript, *Winds of Heaven*, was not liked. We com-
promised, therefore, by using the sub-title. I found also,
that in my effort to write English that would be usual
enough to be acceptable to English speaking people I had

used a number of trite phrases, which I had remembered from English books I had read. In Chinese it is good literary style to use certain well known phrases previously used by great writers. I now learned this is not true in English, and it is best in writing this language to use one's own words. Therefore I went over the manuscript again deleting the phrases I had so painfully put in.

But it was worth the effort, for the little book made its way. Before *The Good Earth* was published, ten months later, *East Wind: West Wind* had become a successful book in its own right, and was in its third printing.

So runs the slight story of *East Wind: West Wind*. The book is of value to me chiefly because it gave me confidence to go on writing, since now I had found a publisher who could be interested in what I wrote, even though I, knowing nothing else well, could write only about China.

JAMES BRANCH CABELL

Born Richmond, Virginia, April 14, 1879.
A.B., William and Mary College, 1898. College instructor, newspaper reporter, coal miner, genealogist. Married. Author: *The Cream of the Jest* (1917), *Jurgen* (1919), *Figures of Earth* (1921). Home: Richmond, Virginia.

RECIPES FOR WRITERS appeared in Part Seven of The Colophon, with special designs by W. A. Dwiggins; September, 1931.

3201 Monument Avenue
Richmond, Virginia
28 December 1936

Dear Mr. Adler:

My first drafts are handwritten and then typed with dejection and many changes. Yet further alterations and additions are made until the page becomes illegible. It is retyped, in the form of two or three pages, after which yet other interlineations are added until this second typing likewise becomes illegible. The process is repeated some three or four times, but by and large the fifth typing proves to be the final copy. I am thus compelled, of course, to do virtually all my own typing.

After the copy is once set in type, I do not, I believe,

A·D·E·F·G·H·I·K·L·M·N·O·J·B·C·P·Q·R·S·T·U·V·W·X·Y·Z

make over-many changes. As to this point, however, my publisher does not always agree with me.

The enclosed typescript is the fourth version of this special passage, which was afterward recopied twice, with some minor changes, before going to the printer.

Yours faithfully,

James Branch Cabell

James Branch Cabell

For one I almost always almost enjoy meeting writers. I like, anyhow, their reliability: and I have known in the flesh a great many writers of varying schools and degrees of talent. At one time or another anybody who has ever written anything appears impelled to visit Richmond: and during the last fifteen years I have thus met I know not how many hundred persons with more or less literary credentials. That which they had printed differed immeasurably. Their work displayed nothing in common, and its fruits clearly emanated from unreticently gifted beings whose minds had not anything in common. What pleased and yet puzzled me too was the fact that as private persons, —inspirited by the second or third Ravished Virgin cocktail, and replete with sandwiches, and seated in the red-covered chair beside my library window,—these writers did all have so very much in common as to convert a conversation with any one of them into a virtually effortless matter.

It were idle to pretend that all the talk made in my library is thus uniformly successful. With the more solid citizenry who now and then get into the room I find social intercourse always to begin unhappily. The trouble is that they take charge of the matter, in their brisk way, by inquiring, with a soul-chilling sprightliness, whether I am writing anything nowadays? This gambit I admire: I have often planned to adapt it so that I myself might begin talk by demanding, say, of a lawyer whether he yet retains his practice, of a clergyman whether he is holding any services nowadays, or of a banker whether his bank is still running; but thus far I have not plucked up the requisite élan. I answer, then, that in point of fact I am at work on a book. They ask (with an appreciably sobered geniality, as of one who had hoped for better tidings) what am I going to call it? When I reply that I have not yet decided, the topic of literature appears exhausted; and conversation has to relapse lumberingly into the more fertile fields of Prohibition and the stock market. But I have never found the least trouble in making talk with my fellow writers.

This happy outcome springs from the fact that all the writers whom I have met in the flesh (and for that matter, I daresay, in the looking-glass) have agreed in their large vanity and in their inexplicable jealousy the one of another. These traits are not to be enregistered as cardinal virtues from the point of view of morality, but in social exercise they work out handsomely. That all-engulfing self-conceit (without which no writer, I most firmly believe, can be worth his salt) affords at once a pleasing topic for conversation. I know that the person opposite really does of necessity consider himself a pre-eminent genius—even in my library, with my Collected Works on full view—and that he requires only to be treated with appropriate deference in the while that we discuss his exploits and revere his books.

The jealousy comes nicely into play the instant that (with the dutifulness of a centurion introducing an Early Christian into the arena) I feed to this lion one or another mention of some other author in terms of artfully mild commendation. The things that a writer can and does very promptly say when any other living writer is tentatively praised continue, even after thirty years of hearing these things, to astonish and delight me. I am spurred to emulousness, and in a while I emule: I draw freely upon my

for my sake, do you consent to avoid temptation. Do you not ever fall into any
this much, like the fine
really serious nature of sin. Come now, do you promise me ~~thatxxiiixxxxx gxxk~~
devil of a fellow that
xfxxiix you are at bottom? and then do you look through your new glasses at this

pxxhxxxxk picture, as our final testing, before you go back to Branlon for your ~~xxxx gxxh~~
allotted while."

~~Well, but Smire lowered the really frightened kitty rather than upset the~~

He charmed eye glasses,
~~xxxxxxxxx~~ Smire said;

¶ "This
~~The~~ picture is like a pink camel lying down. No; it is the map of some

State or another. Why, but to be sure; it is the State of Virginia." ~~Hxxx~~
¶ "But are you ~~xxxx~~ certain of that, Smire?" ¶ "Yes, Company; for its
topography is varied, beginning with the low lying lands along the coast of the
thence rising by
great ~~xxkxxxxy~~ called Chesapeake Bay, known as Tidewater Virginia, and ~~xxxxgxxx~~
inlet,
Piedmont section in the
the extensive tablelands of the ~~Pxxxxxxxxxxgxxxxxxxxgxxx~~ central part of the
way of
commonwealth, to reach mountain elevations up to 5,700 feet in the west. Only,"

own funds of moral indignation, of superior shruggings, and of derogatory hearsay. There is no possibility of the conversation's languishing until the overrated humbug under discussion is quite disposed of to his very last frailty and defect. Then we revert to talking of my visitor's fine work. By-and-by I feed the visitor the name of yet another contemporary writer. And in this way we get on famously.

I have not ever known this simple program to fail. Now and then I have encountered a literary visitor who declined to deviate for one instant in talk from that visitor's own writings even to vilify the works of others, but such stubborn exceptions are rare, and in any case she keeps on talking. And I attend in utter contentment, because I have read of how my own dull eyes and drooping eyelids are informed with intelligence only when I am discoursing upon my own books in a fevered monotony of egotism, varied upon the least provocation by shriek after shriek of wounded vanity. I feel that one who carries the matter to that extreme ought to be patient with the likewise afflicted.

In brief, I almost always almost enjoy talking with writers; nor have I gravely held it against them that during my time they have tended toward broad-mindedness as devastatingly as did the clergy. There has been the difference that to my finding the majority of writers have been proselytizing atheists who have viewed with open acerbity my connections with the church of my fathers. The clergy have seemed merely resigned about it. But all my contemporaries in American letters, so near as I can remember, have from the first embraced agnosticism with deeply religious ardor; they have become zealots of unfaith, very ardently seeking to make converts to all indevotion, and they have seemed to live in an ever-fretful dread of their own not impossible collapse into some form of belief. In this way and in yet other ways they have convinced me that Americans have not learned in my time to be broad-minded with entire ease, no matter how steadfastly throughout the

[39]

last fifteen years we of the literati have tried to achieve the urbane union.

Oncoming antiquaries, I suspect, will not ever give us sophisticated writers of the 'twenties our due credit for the pains with which we learned to converse in drawing-rooms about brothels and privies and homosexuality and syphilis and all other affairs which in our first youth were taboo,— and even as yet we who have reached fifty or thereabouts cannot thus discourse, I am afraid, without some visible effect. I have noted a certain paralytic stiffening of the features (such as a wholly willing martyr might, being human, evince at the first sight of his stake) which gave timely warning that the speaker was now about to approach the obscene with genial levity. Even that fine and strong artist who by common consent discourses bawdily with the most natural gusto, him, too, I have observed a little squeakily to raise his voice in the actual plumping out of each formerly unutterable word whensoever in the presence of ladies he over modestly conveys a general impression of not knowing anybody except bitches and bastards. The effect, in brief, is even here not free, not wholly free, from some visible strain. Yet we stick to it, none the less; and in all such affairs we older writers remain, if anything rather more untiringly broad-minded than are our juniors, in the same conscientious manner.

Moreover so many of the visiting literati have fetched with them to Richmond intense and generally queer looking young women, sometimes under the ægis of free love and sometimes merely as the man's legal wife for the current month, that I too have suffered from the need put upon the creative artist to be fickle and multiversant (and, for choice, priapic) in his amours. I am so eccentric as to lament this need. That the supreme literary court which is composed of the average readers of the average author's books should expect such doings of each fairly successful writer seems fair enough, since it is the comforting salve of the undistinguished citizen to believe that persons of much-talked-about achievement, or of superior social station, are at any rate his inferiors morally. My lament is rather that the artist himself is cowed by this superstition and is driven but too often into flat lechery to defend his genius.

I have known far too many writers who painstakingly honored this creed very much to the hurt of their business in life. Indeed I nowadays look with large wonder upon this onerous superstition and the havoc it has contrived in the doings of innumerous authors whose private affairs are more or less familiar to me,—alluring, as it has done, so many of them to marry indiscriminatingly and repeatedly; leading them (over and above the time squandered by their broad-mindedness in finding extra-legal bedfellows for their wives) to maintain mistresses long after the age when illicit love-affairs have become a nuisance; affording a robust anthology of fairy tales by stirring up a more than antiquarian interest in the old ways of Sodom; quenching all that quietness which is needed to beget a really fine phrase; and in general forcing the American author who in the least respected his repute as a writer very sedulously to avoid the appearance of any bourgeois virtue at the expense of mere reason.

Nor have our sisters in the scribbling trade denied at any rate their lip service to these hidebound conventions. Here of course the affair becomes delicate, and I dare accuse no gifted gentlewoman of continence. I merely remark that, although during the last fifteen years I have in private suspected one or two widely known female writers of personal chastity, he would have been a far bolder man than I who durst twit any one of them with such delinquency in the as yet sophisticated state of American letters.

Now here I think the postman is implicated. Through the postman alone is an author kept in touch with inedited public opinion as it quite honestly regards his writing and his personality. How this affair also may speed with women writers I may not presume to say. I say only that day after day the postman brings to every fairly well known male author an invitation to succor one or another misunderstood wife adulterously and to assuage the carnal loneliness of this or the other unattached spinster: if I forbear to speak of those bright young men who desire (as a rule, in violet ink) to enact Antinoüs to his Hadrian, it is not for lack of subject matter. All these correspondents, then, presuppose the man's sexual piracies so very often, just as an affair of course, that the most unadventurous of penman may well come insensibly to doing that which seems expected of him. In but too many cases this leads to open iniquity such as upsets one's working hours; and after any serious practitioner of the art of writing has mastered his prose style he should be permitted, I think, to live superior to the jogtrot notions of morality.

I would so far honor the conventions that until the man is thirty-five or thereabouts I would bar him from no sort of loose living nor fornication nor crime, although it is better by and large to combine the last-named with an avoidance of the penitentiary. All such misbehaviors will by-and-by be grist to the auctorial mill; they will aid to establish his legend; they content his public; and it is likely the books which he writes meanwhile will not suffer materially, inasmuch as no prose book written before thirty-five is apt to be of relative importance.

But after thirty-five, or by forty at latest, the elect writer has really not the time for the frivolities of broadminded and artistic conduct. He has reached the season wherein, if at all, he must harvest of his baser passions and of his evil doing; even in the teeth of public opinion he may now, I think, avert from sexual immorality with a clear conscience, esteeming it his fairly won privilege to lead that sober and immured life wherein alone he may find full opportunity to pursue his sedentary trade. It has now become

[42]

his main duty to write, and to give over all to his art, without any further corporal truckling to the vices which his constitution is no longer able to support with distinction. Nor will his fair repute suffer by this in the long run, provided only that his writings survive him; the vicarious lecheries and the mental masturbations of the professors who will edit his remains may be safely counted upon to provide the final years of his biography with the requisite misbehavior.

Meanwhile it occurs to me that these observations as to the natural history of prose writers may be robbed of any large significance by the fact that I may have encountered no authors of profound or enduring worth. About that I of course do not know. For one matter it has been the fate of my prolonged diversion, in the Biography of the life of Manuel, to fare always an appreciable way apart from the fields wherein my contemporaries were at play; our interests were not ever quite the same; and as one result of this I have very often applauded my confrères with a certain conscious lack of sympathy. I perceived their manifold merits, that is, perforce and with a rather distasteful clarity. There has always been present, just around the corner, the notion that if these so obviously talented persons were selecting their themes and the proper treatment of them with intelligence, then I must be making of myself, in my Poictesmes and my Lichfields, a spectacle which I preferred not to consider.

It has followed—no doubt, as a result of this very ugly and unworthy notion—that even nowadays I do not regard any one of my contemporaries quite so seriously as to believe that during my time Shakespeare and the Bible have been hopelessly dispossessed from their rumored supremacy in our literature. Yet I admit too that every current book is unfairly handicapped by its manifest failure to be the book which the publishers describe on the dust jacket:

and I know that each era has overmodestly believed itself to be bereft of literary genius.

This belief is not wholly due, perhaps, to the polite pretense of every reviewer that the especial author upon whom he is now operating is the reviewer's equal. I suspect the author may be far more to blame, in that he only too often permits his reviewers, and even his potential readers, to see him and to know him personally. He does not with a shrewd humbleness remember that, in the judicious words of Trelawny, "to know an author personally is to destroy the illusion created by his works; if you withdraw the veil of your idol's sanctuary, and see him in his nightcap, you discover a querulous old crone, a sour pedant, a supercilious coxcomb, a servile tuft-hunter, a saucy snob, or, at best, an ordinary mortal."

Edward John Trelawny had known a number of admittedly great authors: and I think that he spoke the truth as to every gifted writer who is yet alive. Living, the writer who has genius gets hourly in the way of his own ability and obscures it. Living, he does but too often, and far too willingly, illustrate what Keats meant by his cryptic saying, "Of all God's creatures a poet is the most unpoetical." Living, he exhibits, not merely in my library but to his beholders at large, that childlike yet that wholly necessary self-conceit and that vivacious jealousy as to which I have spoken: and he in many other ways, and upon every possible occasion, arouses strong doubts as to his exact mental balance.

Yet every writer of fiction comes among us, let it be remembered, from out of a land in which he is God: he comes from a very high ordaining of love and death and of all human affairs in this more familiar land, which his characters inhabit, to make civil talk for us in our trim drawing-rooms or to foster those more hardy platitudes which alone may flourish upon the bleak lecture platform. We should always remember in our dealings with literary

people that each author is in every essential a foreigner but
lately emigrated from the one land which is comprehensible
to him; and that also he goes among us perforce in a half-
sleep, preserving as best the poor man can the amenities of
our physical dreamland by pretending to believe in us. So
does he become ludicrous in our eyes, because he perceives
only too plainly that no one of us is an important or an enduring phenomenon. And about the importance and the
enduringness of that world wherein he is God—here also—
he may of course be quite right, provided only he has made
the grave error of being born a genius.

For this reason I often wonder if ever among these
visiting literati I have encountered authentic genius as it
went incognito, veiled by the rude requirements of food
and pocket money and yet other fleshly foibles. It well may
be that this exceedingly boring person, or this seemingly
insane person, will bulk largely in to-morrow's literature,
with a Life and Letters and a very dull host of commenta-
tors. The circumstance may even be mentioned, in his
Authorized Biography, that on such and such a date he
was in Richmond and then visited me, with a footnote to
explain who I was. Each visitor who comes me-ward may
be that predestined person; I have no possible way of tell-
ing; and with the eternal survival of my full name and ad-
dress (at least, perhaps) thus inexpensively purchasable, I
find that I almost always almost enjoy meeting writers.

CHARLES WADDELL CHESNUTT

Born Cleveland, Ohio, June 20, 1858.

Married Miss Susan U. Perry at the age of twenty. For nine years he taught in the public schools of North Carolina, and at the age of twenty-three became principal of the State Normal School in Fayetteville. In 1884 he spent some months writing for the New York newspapers, and three years later was admitted to the Ohio bar. Author: *The Conjure Woman* (1899), *The Wife of His Youth and Other Stories* (1899), *Life of Frederick Douglass* (1899), *The House Behind the Cedars* (1900), *The Marrow of Tradition* (1901), *The Colonel's Dream* (1905). Died, November 15, 1932, at Cleveland.

Post-Bellum — Pre-Harlem appeared in Part Five of The Colophon: February, 1931.

15417 Lucknow Ave.
Cleveland, Ohio
December 29, 1936

My dear Mr. Adler:

My mother has asked me to answer the letter which she received from you last week.

My father always wrote his copy by hand, although he was an expert shorthand writer and typist. He used any paper that

[47]

A·B·D·E·F·G·H·I·J·K·L·M·**C·W·C**·N·O·P·Q·R·S·T·U·V·X·Y·Z

came to hand. His manuscripts are made up of papers of all shapes and sizes.

After the original copy written by hand was finished he would have it typed (in his younger days he typed it himself) and then would rewrite it and make many changes on the typed copy. Often many copies were made before he was satisfied.

After the copy was set in type he made very few changes. I have some page proof here with scarcely a correction.

Practically all of Mr. Chesnutt's creative work was done after business hours. He followed his profession of court reporter throughout his life except for two years in about 1900 and 1901, when he devoted himself exclusively to literary work. In that period he did a great deal of lecturing and reading, and much writing, but the needs of a growing family, the education of four children—two at Smith, one at Harvard, and one at Western Reserve—made it imperative that he earn more money than his literary work produced. So at the end of the two years, his literary work again took second place.

I am sending you some characteristic copy. It is part of the original copy of The House Behind the Cedars. *Along with it you will find the first typed copy with the changes and corrections which he made. You can thus see how he changed the copy after it had been typed.*

I hope that this information is satisfactory to you, and that the copy that I am sending will prove adequate. If not, please let me know.

Sincerely yours,

Helen M. Chesnutt

Charles W. Chesnutt

My FIRST BOOK, *The Conjure Woman*, was published by the Houghton Mifflin Company in 1899. It was not, strictly speaking, a novel, though it has been so called, but a collection of short stories in Negro dialect, put in the mouth of an old Negro gardener, and related by him in each instance to the same audience, which consisted of the Northern lady and gentleman who employed him. They are naïve and simple stories, dealing with alleged incidents of chattel slavery, as the old man had known it and as I had heard of it, and centering around the professional activities of old Aunt Peggy, the plantation conjure woman, and others of that ilk.

In every instance Julius had an axe to grind, for himself or his church, or some member of his family, or a white friend. The introductions to the stories, which were written in the best English I could command, developed the characters of Julius's employers and his own, and the wind-up of each story reveals the old man's ulterior purpose, which, as a general thing, is accomplished.

Most of the stories in *The Conjure Woman* had appeared in the *Atlantic Monthly* from time to time, the first story, *The Goophered Grapevine*, in the issue of August, 1887, and one of them, *The Conjurer's Revenge*, in the *Overland Monthly*. Two of them were first printed in the bound volume.

After the book had been accepted for publication, a friend of mine, the late Judge Madison W. Beacon, of

Cleveland, a charter member of the Rowfant Club, suggested to the publishers a limited edition, which appeared in advance of the trade edition in an issue of one hundred and fifty numbered copies and was subscribed for almost entirely by members of the Rowfant Club and of the Cleveland bar. It was printed by the Riverside Press on large hand-made linen paper, bound in yellow buckram, with the name on the back in black letters on a white label, a very handsome and dignified volume. The trade edition was bound in brown cloth and on the front was a picture of a white-haired old Negro, flanked on either side by a long-eared rabbit. The dust-jacket bore the same illustration.

The name of the story teller, "Uncle" Julius, and the locale of the stories, as well as the cover design, were suggestive of Mr. Harris's *Uncle Remus*, but the tales are entirely different. They are sometimes referred to as folk tales, but while they employ much of the universal machinery of wonder stories, especially the metamorphosis, with one exception, that of the first story, "The Goophered Grapevine," of which the norm was a folk tale, the stories are the fruit of my own imagination, in which respect they differ from the *Uncle Remus* stories which are avowedly folk tales.

Several subsequent editions of *The Conjure Woman* were brought out; just how many copies were sold altogether I have never informed myself, but not enough for the royalties to make me unduly rich, and in 1929, just thirty years after the first appearance of the book, a new edition was issued by Houghton Mifflin Company. It was printed from the original plates, with the very handsome title page of the limited edition, an attractive new cover in black and red, and a very flattering foreword by Colonel Joel Spingarn.

Most of my books are out of print, but I have been told that it is quite unusual for a volume of short stories which is not one of the accepted modern classics to remain on sale for so long a time.

At the time when I first broke into print seriously, no American colored writer had ever secured critical recognition except Paul Laurence Dunbar, who had won his laurels as a poet. Phillis Wheatley, a Colonial poet, had gained recognition largely because she was a slave and born in Africa, but the short story, or the novel of life and manners, had not been attempted by any one of that group.

There had been many novels dealing with slavery and the Negro. Harriet Beecher Stowe, especially in *Uncle Tom's Cabin*, had covered practically the whole subject of slavery and race admixture. George W. Cable had dwelt upon the romantic and some of the tragic features of racial contacts in Louisiana, and Judge Albion W. Tourgee, in what was one of the best sellers of his day, *A Fool's Errand*, and in his *Bricks Without Straw*, had dealt with the problems of reconstruction.

Thomas Dixon was writing the Negro down industriously and with marked popular success. Thomas Nelson Page was disguising the harshness of slavery under the mask of sentiment. The trend of public sentiment at the moment was distinctly away from the Negro. He had not developed any real political or business standing; socially he was outcast. His musical and stage successes were still for the most part unmade, and on the whole he was a small frog in a large pond, and there was a feeling of pessimism in regard to his future.

Publishers are human, and of course influenced by the opinions of their public. The firm of Houghton Mifflin, however, was unique in some respects. One of the active members of the firm was Francis J. Garrison, son of William Lloyd Garrison, from whom he had inherited his father's hatred of slavery and friendliness to the Negro. His partner, George H. Mifflin, was a liberal and generous gentleman trained in the best New England tradition. They were both

A·B·D·E·F·G·H·I·J·K·L·M·C·W·C·N·O·P·Q·R·S·T·U·V·X·Y·Z

friendly to my literary aspirations and became my personal friends.

But the member of their staff who was of most assistance to me in publishing my first book was Walter Hines Page, later ambassador to England under President Wilson, and at that time editor of the *Atlantic Monthly*, as well as literary adviser for the publishing house, himself a liberalized Southerner, who derived from the same part of the South where the stories in *The Conjure Woman* are located, and where I passed my adolescent years. He was a graduate of Macon College, a fellow of Johns Hopkins University, had been attached to the staff of the *Forum* and the *New York Evening Post*, and was as broad-minded a Southerner as it was ever my good fortune to meet.

Three of the *Atlantic* editors wrote novels dealing with race problems—William Dean Howells in *An Imperative Duty*, Bliss Perry in *The Plated City*, and Mr. Page in *The Autobiography of Nicholas Worth*.

The first of my conjure stories had been accepted for the *Atlantic* by Thomas Bailey Aldrich, the genial auburn-haired poet who at that time presided over the editorial desk. My relations with him, for the short time they lasted, were most cordial and friendly.

Later on I submitted to Mr. Page several stories of post-war life among the colored people which the *Atlantic* published, and still later the manuscript of a novel. The novel was rejected, and was subsequently rewritten and published by Houghton Mifflin under the title of *The House Behind the Cedars*. Mr. Page, who had read the manuscript, softened its rejection by the suggestion that perhaps a collection of the conjure stories might be undertaken by the firm with a better prospect of success. I was in the hands of my friends, and submitted the collection. After some omissions and additions, all at the advice of Mr. Page, the book was accepted and announced as *The Conjure Woman*, in 1899, and I enjoyed all the delights of proof-reading and the other pleasant emotions attending the publication of a first book. Mr. Page, Mr. Garrison and Mr. Mifflin vied with each other in helping to make our joint venture a literary and financial success.

The book was favorably reviewed by literary critics. If I may be pardoned one quotation, William Dean Howells, always the friend of the aspiring author, in an article published in the *Atlantic Monthly* for May, 1900, wrote:

"The stories of *The Conjure Woman* have a wild, indigenous poetry, the creation of sincere and original imagination, which is imparted with a tender humorousness and a very artistic reticence. As far as his race is concerned, or his sixteenth part of a race, it does not greatly matter whether Mr. Chesnutt invented their motives, or found them, as he feigns, among his distant cousins of the Southern cabins. In either case the wonder of their beauty is the same, and whatever is primitive and sylvan or campestral in the reader's heart is touched by the spells thrown on the simple black lives in these enchanting tales. Character, the most precious thing in fiction, is faithfully portrayed."

Imagine the thrill with which a new author would read such an encomium from such a source!

From the publisher's standpoint, the book proved a modest success. This was by no means a foregone conclusion, even assuming its literary merit and the publisher's imprint, for reasons which I shall try to make clear.

I have been referred to as the "first Negro novelist," meaning, of course, in the United States; Pushkin in Russia and the two Dumas in France had produced a large body of popular fiction. At that time a literary work by an American of acknowledged color was a doubtful experiment, both for the writer and for the publisher, entirely apart from its intrinsic merit. Indeed, my race was never mentioned by the publishers in announcing or advertising the book. From my own viewpoint it was a personal matter. It never occurred to me to claim any merit because of it, and I have always resented the denial of anything on account of it. My colored friends, however, with a very natural and laudable zeal for the race, with which I found no fault, saw to it that the fact was not overlooked, and I have before me a copy of a letter written by one of them to the editor of the *Atlanta Constitution*, which had published a favorable review of the book, accompanied by my portrait, chiding him because the reviewer had not referred to my color.

A woman critic of Jackson, Mississippi, questioning what she called the rumor as to my race, added, "Some people claim that Alexander Dumas, author of *The Count of Monte Cristo* and *The Three Musketeers*, was a colored man. This is obviously untrue, because no Negro could possibly have written these books"—a pontifical announcement which would seem to settle the question definitely, despite the historical evidence to the contrary.

While *The Conjure Woman* was in the press, the *Atlantic* published a short story of mine called "The Wife of His Youth" which attracted wide attention. James McArthur, at that time connected with the *Critic*, later with *Harper's*, in talking one day with Mr. Page, learned of my race and requested leave to mention it as a matter of interest to the literary public. Mr. Page demurred at first on the ground that such an announcement might be harmful to the success of my forthcoming book, but finally consented, and Mr. McArthur mentioned the fact in the *Critic*, referring to me as a "mulatto."

As a matter of fact, substantially all of my writings, with the exception of *The Conjure Woman*, have dealt with the problems of people of mixed blood, which, while in the main the same as those of the true Negro, are in some instances and in some respects much more complex and difficult of treatment, in fiction as in life.

I have lived to see, after twenty years or more, a marked change in the attitude of publishers and the read-

occasion to see him on legal business in relation to her little

property.   She had always ~~behaved~~ behaved himself with a ~~depreciating~~ sort of dig-

nity, and he had always treated her with respect;- ~~no respect~~ neither the dignity nor
the respect were quite the real thing, but enough so for the purposes
~~of such intercourse as they had.~~ in the woman's story. There went neareno, too, connected with the
consciousel transferred to her some of the feeling he had in a con
mind of the old friend alone referred to why he should treat the woman
kindly, and clerk of his youth.   The boy was his mother's son, of course,
~~But he was also his father's child, and this the old~~ carefully although he had not cared to mention a namethat he did not hear.
~~If. The old judge's mind reverted to~~
~~II.~~   thought of certain laws and judicial decisions he once or twice in his lifetime.

had had occasion to look up ~~a short time before~~

"Why not?" he asked, speaking to himself this time, rather than

to the boy.   But a footfall sounded in the outer office, and a

client appeared in the doorway, a female client, at sight of whom the
~~boy withdrew. He knew she would spend the morning tacking over~~
~~of matters that the judge knew were impertinent detail~~
"Why not?" he said, addressing the boy. "Come and see me at

eight o'clock tomorrow morning, and I'll tell you, if not, why not. Good
morning, Mrs. Carter. I see I see you well this morning, "

ing public in regard to the Negro in fiction. The development of Harlem, with its large colored population in all shades, from ivory to ebony, of all degrees of culture, from doctors of philosophy to the lowest grade of illiteracy; its various origins, North American, South American, West Indian and African; its morals ranging from the highest to the most debased; with the vivid life of its cabarets, dance halls, and theatres; with its ambitious business and professional men, its actors, singers, novelists and poets, its aspirations and demands for equality—without which any people would merit only contempt—presented a new field for literary exploration which of recent years has been cultivated assiduously.

One of the first of the New York writers to appreciate the possibilities of Harlem for literary purposes was Carl Van Vechten, whose novel *Nigger Heaven* was rather severely criticized by some of the colored intellectuals as a libel on the race, while others of them praised it highly. I was prejudiced in its favor for reasons which those who have read the book will understand. I found it a vivid and interesting story which presented some new and better types of Negroes and treated them sympathetically.

The Negro novel, whether written by white or colored authors, has gone so much farther now in the respects in which it was criticized that *Nigger Heaven*, in comparison with some of these later productions, would be almost as mild as a Sunday School tract compared to *The Adventures of Fanny Hill*. Several of these novels, by white and colored authors alike, reveal such an intimate and meticulous familiarity with the baser aspects of Negro life, North and South, that one is inclined to wonder how and from what social sub-sewers they gathered their information. With the exception of one or two of the earlier ones, the heroine of the novel is never chaste, though for the matter of that few post-Victorian heroines are, and most of the male characters are likewise weaklings or worse.

[55]

I have in mind a recent novel, brilliantly written by a gifted black author, in which, to my memory, there is not a single decent character, male or female. These books are written primarily for white readers, as it is extremely doubtful whether a novel, however good, could succeed financially on its sales to colored readers alone. But it seems to me that a body of twelve million people, struggling upward slowly but surely from a lowly estate, must present all along the line of its advancement many situations full of dramatic interest, ranging from farce to tragedy, with many admirable types worthy of delineation.

Caste, a principal motive of fiction from Richardson down through the Victorian epoch, has pretty well vanished among white Americans. Between the whites and the Negroes it is acute, and is bound to develop an increasingly difficult complexity, while among the colored people themselves it is just beginning to appear.

Negro writers no longer have any difficulty in finding publishers. Their race is no longer a detriment but a good selling point, and publishers are seeking their books, sometimes, I am inclined to think, with less regard for quality than in the case of white writers. To date, colored writers have felt restricted for subjects to their own particular group, but there is every reason to hope that in the future, with proper encouragement, they will make an increasingly valuable contribution to literature, and perhaps produce chronicles of life comparable to those of Dostoevski, Dumas, Dickens or Balzac.

A. E. COPPARD

Born Folkestone, England, January 4, 1878.
Educated at Lewes Road Board School, but left at the age
of nine because of ill health. Worked as professional
printer and clerk. Author *Adam & Eve & Pinch Me* (1921),
Clorinda Walks in Heaven (1922), *Silver Circus* (1928), *Pink
Furniture* (1930). Home: Long Wittenham, Abingdon, Berk-
shire, England.

ON FIRST GETTING INTO PRINT appeared in
Part Six of The Colophon; June, 1931.

Walberswick, Southwold
Suffolk, England
1-1-37

Dear Mr. Adler   re "Getting into Print"

I always compose my tales by hand, first in pencil and
generally in a school exercise book. After that I make corrections in
ink. When I am satisfied I write out a fair copy in ink for typing.
Altho I can type fairly well I have never composed directly on a
typewriter—that is a mode quite beyond the reach of my under-
standing. (Once on a time I used to compose on the back of the
typescript of rejected manuscripts.)

The final MS is generally typed by myself, tho I oc-
casionally employ a typist.

[57]

B·D·F·G·H·I·J·K·L·M·N·O·A·E·C·P·Q·R·S·T·U·V·W·X·Y·Z

I have never been able to dictate.

One printer's proof is sufficient.

Only trifling changes are made. I could not send a tale to a printer until I thought it completely "finished."

Specimens attached.

Yours sincerely

A. E. Coppard

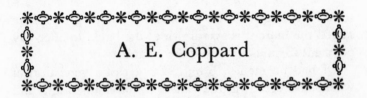

A. E. Coppard

To the young and confident scribe the difficulties of first getting into print seem incomprehensible, and his bewilderment is not lessened as he observes the emergence into print of what does emerge, the appearance of what does appear. To a new writer who has faith in himself, by which I suppose I am bound to mean ninety-nine and a half out of every hundred new writers, this astounding neglect of his own in favour of other people's manuscripts—manuscripts which are rackety with symptoms of imaginative neuralgia and pennywise profundity—seems due rather to editorial malice than to the myopia of incompetence.

It is too flattering a defence to blame the lowness of public taste. The public rightly wants the best it can get for its money, and has no general level of taste. It may be argued that its standards are made for it by editorial design, and the public has to endure what the editorial intelligence provides. On the other hand there certainly are some editors of genius, though what with their directors, their advertisers, their writers, their circulation and their readers, they have an uncomfortable time.

Of course it is not difficult to get into print if you have money and can afford to pay for publication—there have been some great books published in this way, Samuel Butler's for instance—or if you are acquainted with any of those magazines which make a virtue of their deficits and consider it impure in the cause of art, which grows more sacred the more it is overdrawn at the bank, to offer any payment to anybody—even the printer.

I had no money to burn, but I cast a good deal of wholesome bread on the waters of unremunerating and unremunerative magazines, and I declare that every such piece has been republished in volumes of mine, with the sole exception of some verses called "Wishes." These wishes were first fatuously expressed in a periodical called *Coterie*, run by an Indian student at Oxford, Chaman Lal, a very agreeable fellow who has since become a figure in Indian politics.

But what made me write? What is it that makes any-one write at all? I mean, apart from the need of money or the desire for some sort of repute, what is the original compulsion? H. G. Wells somewhere says: "Every true artist, so far as his art went, has always got out of himself—has forgotten his personal interests and become Man thinking for the whole race." It is a very intriguing suggestion, but the sort of writer I am could lay no claim to such high destiny. I do not know what made me begin to write fiction and verse, unless it was that always having been a great reader my imitative faculties grew especially along those lines. As a child I gorged myself on Buffalo Bill, Deadwood Dick, Calamity Jane, and all that halfpenny library of the wild woolly West which so enchanted youth in the eighties and nineties of the last century; its aroma and atmosphere engendered a nostalgia that has never left me, and when, long after I became a writer, I met an American from Montana who had known Jack London, I was awed as if I had met one of the twelve apostles. Yet I never had any liking for Bret Harte's tales. In my teens I got hold of one or two Dickens and a cheap complete Shakespeare, but at twenty I was given over to the reading of poetry and the study of fine art with a fond determination to write poetry myself. And I could not. I could *not* write poetry, not even

Cockney ~~fellows they were,~~

Here they were these 2 low felows, ~~wealthy~~ from Parders End
somewhere down Lder way the sort nobody'd care to meet in
broad of day let alone a night ~~them~~ like as I was then. They were
~~bound for~~ up north some place right to Greenock or some mining hole to
~~mark —~~ ~~they never came out~~ actually where, so but it was a long
ways from Parders End + they'd been going a week with
no more than a dollar between 'em.   Beager, the little of
them one, was ~~begged~~ liable to fits any time with no more warning a draftsway dout to ~~fling year~~ for his marks, + Billie Braun, the other, was a walking menace one of those blunge bellobbing husky with long
sides that never ~~save~~ gave out, + ~~ugly~~ and the whole or other of em not nice to
be about, at all ~~telling of 'em~~.

~~They were off of with north some place of eighththe~~

They'd begged food at houses + money from hard faces, + all
a long now way on. Sometimes they got it, + other sometimes
they didn't. When they didn't Beager we life into some little
acers an age of buy a packet of fags + had left a tin of corned
~~beef or something~~ frogs akron + anybody, like that gayog hands, + so they carried
a bosky till they got into Nottingshire + a Nottingshire + nothing towards
Scotland Course didn't go any more than they cd help
~~north that~~ into Re big towns, of which a have

badly. One day my friend Tom Olliver said to me: "You are wrong to spend all your time reading poetry; you ought to read some prose, modern prose." He was an attendant at a little circulating library in Brighton and offered to lend me a book or two, on the quiet, out of his boss's stock. So on a Whitmonday, somewhere about the end of the last century—holy and sacred medallion, how the time goes!— on this Whitmonday he brought me a book of stories to read, but I didn't look at it then because we and half a dozen other fellows were just going off for a day's ramble on the South Downs. I remember I kept on playing on a mouth-organ the only two tunes I could manage; one was "Sweet Rosy O'Grady," which Masefield misquotes in *Sard Harker*. I masticated these two melodies until all the other fellows got mad, and then we came to the village of Poynings, where we all got a little drunk. I can't remember much else about that day on the downs except that I kept getting at loggerheads with a lanky fellow, Ernie, who loathed me, but when I got home at night there was Tom's book for me to read. It was *Life's Little Ironies* by Thomas Hardy. I remember I read the first tale and wept, pleasurable tears, mournful tears, perhaps drunken tears, over its tragic beauty. It is called "A Son's Veto," and I still think it one of the most moving stories in the world. When I had finished the book it was clear to me that my real mission in life was to write not poetry any more but short stories. It was an ambition that I nourished in secret for over twelve years. No, it is wrong to say "nourished," for I made not the slightest effort to realize it. I might have been a flower-pot in which was buried a bulb that had neither power nor inclination to put forth a single shoot. But the bulb, whether worthless or not, was not dead. I was always declaring to myself: "I am going to write short stories, some day I am going to write short stories. I am going to!" Heaven and earth! the abysses into which human confidence may topple us. I was like those policemen who are going, very soon, to tackle the Pirates of Penzance. They burst into a long chant, with the refrain, "We go! We go! We go!" and they continue this chant so long that at last the exasperated Major cries: "Ah, but damn it, you *don't* go!"

Somewhere about 1912, when I was working as a clerk in Oxford, I wrote my first story. It was twelve thousand words long and I called it "Fleet." In a mood of what seems like effrontery to me now I despatched this immature effort to *The English Review*, at that time a power in the literary world. To my chagrin Mr. Austin Harrison declined it! It was too long, he said, it was not the sort of fiction he required, but he would like to see anything else I had to show. I had nothing else; but I wrote another tale, and then another, both of which I refrained from submitting to anybody. They were all "too long," I was sure, and so I buried the three of them in some domestic limbo where they have since, I hope, been devoured by mice or succumbed to some fungus. I determined to write much shorter things, and one of the first results was "Weep Not, My Wanton," which I submitted to *The New Statesman*, at that time edited by Mr. J. C. Squire. He sent it back with a card to say that the title was "very neat." For a long time after that I did not send out any more manuscripts to editors, I just went on writing and accumulating a store of tales until I had six or seven. In the year 1916 a university magazine called *The Isis*, or it may have been *The Varsity*, edited by T. W. Earp whom I knew personally, printed my little tale, "Communion," and this was the first appearance in print of any tale of mine, though I fancy it was in the same year that a journal called *The Egoist*, edited by T. S. Eliot, printed two pieces of my *vers libre*. But the first thing for which I received any payment—and that is surely the circumstance from which one begins to date—was "Piffingcap," which caught the eye of the editor of *Pearson's Magazine* and was printed in a special George Robey number in July, 1918. Having just then more than a dozen

B·D·F·G·H·I·J·K·L·M·N·O·A·E·C·P·Q·R·S·T·U·V·W·X·Y·Z

tales finished I had suddenly sent the whole lot out singly
to different magazines. I was lucky enough to get three ac-
ceptances, "Piffingcap," "Weep Not, My Wanton" for *The
Saturday Westminster*, and "Dusky Ruth" which *The English
Review* printed in November of that year. I felt pleased,
even excited, to be in *Pearson's* and the *Westminster*, but my
sensations on getting into *The English Review* were entirely
godlike. It was still the great literary monthly of the time,
though the war had nearly ruined it, and my repute among
my friends was enhanced amazingly by this achievement.
Pearson's had given me five pounds on acceptance. That
was good and amiable, five pounds was five pounds, but
The English Review . . . ! Ah, I anticipated a really stout
cheque from them. But so many months went by after the
appearance of "Dusky Ruth" that at last I had to write to
the editor and remind him of my claim. To my horror he
answered that the *Review* was in a bad way and could
afford no more than the three and a half guineas which he
apologetically enclosed. It was a great blow, for at the end
of the war I had abandoned the frying-pan of office life and
jumped into the stove of a "literary career." I had expected
at least ten pounds! I wrote and thanked poor Austin Harrison, but I remember hinting that his scale of remunera-
tion would scarcely keep my wife in hairpins. Or perhaps
I said that a year later, after he had printed "Pomona's
Babe!" Poor man, I should like to have met him before he
died; he gave me a great deal of encouragement, even
though he did nearly put me into liquidation!

At the beginning of 1919 I had enough tales to make
up into a volume, which I called *Adam & Eve & Pinch Me*,
and I tried them on many publishers, including Methuen,
Macmillan, Constable, Chatto and Windus, Heinemann,
Grant Richards, and Ward, Lock & Co., but none of them
took a fancy to me. Most of them had the same excuse—
that volumes of short stories were not in demand and did

not pay to publish. Others said they were not suitable, and one or two invited me to submit a novel.

This period of tribulation lasted nearly two years, when my manuscripts had reached Messrs. Nisbet's in their rounds, and owing to the good offices of Louis Golding stood a fair chance of acceptance by them. Then one day, while I was upstairs mending my trousers, I heard a voice at my cottage door. I put on my trousers and went downstairs to confront a tall pale young man in spectacles. He turned out to be Harold Taylor, who was then organising The Golden Cockerel Press, a new sort of co-operative publishing society, and wanted to begin publishing on the first of April, 1921. He had read a story of mine "Arabesque" in a non-paying magazine called *Voices*, run by Thomas Moult. And that, by the way, is a magazine in which you will find the early work of a number of writers who have made reputations since its day. I gladly pay my tribute to *Voices*, for it brought Harold Taylor to my door. He had been impressed by that story of mine, and had cycled nearly forty miles to ask if I had a number of such tales which he could issue in a volume to inaugurate his new press with! Had I not! Had I not, indeed! We spent a very entertaining day together, and it ended by my writing off at once to Messrs. Nisbet, asking for the return of my manuscripts. A few days later Taylor had begun on them, and in due course, on that auspicious date, *Adam & Eve & Pinch Me* appeared.

Taylor's press was to embody some co-operative ideals he was keen on, and I remember that I did some odd journeyman work in his printing room, such as inking the rollers, feeding the paper, helping to bind, printing labels, packing and such like. Later on in the year when Taylor was ill, a small boy and I printed off 18,000 sheets of some book. I fancy it was Martin Armstrong's.

From all this it will be seen that sheer luck played a big part in my progress to book form, just as it has played a part in making that book a collector's rarity. For *Adam & Eve & Pinch Me* was a pretty poor specimen of book production, no one with the eye of anything but a cod could deny it; poor Taylor himself was most caustic about it, it was a marvel that the covers retained the embrace of the sheets for even twenty-four hours. Taylor never did so badly again—it would indeed have been difficult—and perhaps its present rarity may be attributed to the inevitable collapse of many copies.

THEODORE DREISER

Born Terre Haute, Indiana, August 27, 1871.
Attended University of Indiana for one year. Worked on
newspapers and magazines, and was, from 1907 to 1910,
editor-in-chief of the Butterick Publications. Organized
the National Child Rescue Campaign, 1907. Married.
Author *Sister Carrie* (1900), *Jennie Gerhardt* (1911), *The
Genius* (1915), *An American Tragedy* (1925). Home: Mount
Kisco, New York.

THE EARLY ADVENTURES OF "SISTER
CARRIE" appeared in Part Five of The Colophon;
February, 1931.

December 31, 1936
50 West 77th St.
New York City

Dear Mr. Adler,

Mr. Dreiser has your letter of the 21st, and here are the
answers to some of your questions.

As a rule Mr. Dreiser writes in longhand. Years ago
he did use a typewriter for a time but gave that up as he found that
it was easier for him to write by hand. Once in a while he dictates
the copy. He gets someone else to do the typing and then he makes
corrections and changes on the typed copy.

Also, he makes many changes and corrections on the printers' proofs so that often he has to have several proofs.

Just at present Mr. Dreiser has no characteristic copy which he could give you to reproduce.

I hope that this covers the information you desire.

Yours sincerely

Harriet Bissell
Secretary

Theodore Dreiser

I AM FREQUENTLY asked for the story of the trials and tribulations attendant upon the publication of my first novel—*Sister Carrie*. The interest of the story to me at this time lies in the picture it presents of the moral taboos of that day as reflected by publishing conditions that made possible such an experience as mine in connection with *Sister Carrie*.

When I first turned to writing it was mainly articles for magazines that occupied my attention. But having no such "happy" stories to tell as those that filled the pages of the popular magazines of the day, I met with little success. My own reactions to life were so diametrically opposed to the fiction of that time. I then turned to a novel, beginning its first pages in the autumn of 1899 and finishing it in May, 1900. But even with the novel finished, I found little encouragement. I took it first to Henry Mills Alden, editor of *Harper's Magazine*, who read the manuscript and, while expressing approval, at the same time doubted whether any publisher would take it. The American mass mind of that day, as he knew, was highly suspicious of any truthful interpretation of life. However, he turned it over to Harper & Brothers, who kept it three weeks and then informed me that they could not publish it.

I next submitted it to Doubleday, Page, where Frank Norris occupied the position of reader. He recommended it most enthusiastically to his employers, and it seemed

A·B·C·E·F·G·H·I·J·K·L·M·T·D·N·O·P·Q·R·S·U·V·W·X·Y·Z

that my book was really to be published, for a few weeks later I signed a contract with Doubleday Page and the book was printed.

In the meantime (as I was told by Frank Norris himself, and later by William Heinemann, the publisher, of London), Mrs. Frank Doubleday read the manuscript and was horrified by its frankness. She was a social worker and active in moral reform, and because of her strong dislike for the book and insistence that it be withdrawn from publication, Doubleday, Page decided not to put it in circulation. However, Frank Norris remained firm in his belief that the book should come before the American public, and persuaded me to insist on the publishers carrying out the contract. Their legal adviser—one Thomas McKee, who afterwards personally narrated to me his share in all this—was called in, and he advised the firm that it was legally obliged to go on with the publication, it having signed a contract to do so, but that this did not necessarily include *selling*; in short, the books, after publication, might be thrown into the cellar! I believe this advice was followed to the letter, because no copies were ever sold. But Frank Norris, as he himself told me, did manage to send out some copies to book reviewers, probably a hundred of them.

After some five years, I induced J. F. Taylor & Company, rare book dealers, to undertake the publication of *Sister Carrie* providing I would precede it with a new novel. My intention was to furnish them with *Jennie Gerhardt*, but my health being poor I could not complete it. In the meantime the plates of *Sister Carrie* and some bound and unbound copies had been purchased by them for five hundred dollars or thereabouts. Later, having turned to editorial work, I laid up sufficient to repurchase the plates and copies and thereafter—until the reissue of the work by B. W. Dodge Company—the same remained in my possession, and still do.

In 1901 *Sister Carrie* was published by Heinemann in London and gained considerable publicity. Acting on this, I took the manuscript (in 1907, when I was editor of the Butterick publications) to the then newly formed publishing house of B. W. Dodge Company, who brought the book out in that year. In 1908 Grosset & Dunlap published *Sister Carrie*, using the same plates, but even at that day the outraged protests far outnumbered the plaudits. Later, in 1911, it was reissued by Harper & Brothers, who had just published *Jennie Gerhardt*. Still later, after John Lane had thrown me out on account of *The "Genius,"* it was taken over by Boni & Liveright and published. That was in 1917. And there its harried and varied wanderings ended.

JOSEPH HERGESHEIMER

Born Philadelphia, Pennsylvania, February 15, 1880.
Educated at a Quaker school and at Pennsylvania Academy of Fine Arts. Married 1907, Miss Dorothy Hemphill,
who signed her husband's first published work. Author
The Three Black Pennys (1917), *Cytherea* (1922), *The Bright
Shawl* (1922), *Sheridan* (1931). Home: The Dower House,
West Chester, Pennsylvania.

BIOGRAPHY AND BIBLIOGRAPHIES appeared
in Part Eight of The Colophon; December, 1931.

The Dower House
West Chester, Pa.
8 February 1937

Mr. Hergesheimer answers:

[*1*] *First writes out notes by hand.*

[*2*] *They are typed by secretary.*

[*3*] *Corrects galley and page proofs.*

[*4*] *Makes no changes.*

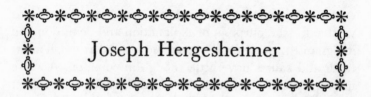

Joseph Hergesheimer

BIOGRAPHY, it seems, has come to have as many devices as there are forms of the dying novel. There are biographies of men and women and of times and places. Partisan biographies, dogmatic works and exercises in atmosphere. Especially exercises in atmosphere. As thin. The descriptions of places, the re-creation of historical periods —the easiest, perhaps, of all to write—include every privilege of the imagination once the property of fiction. Imagination and indignation now appear to be the most evident qualities of biography. The writer of a biography, for example, selects an era when, obviously, a great injustice was worked—the reconstruction period following the Civil War in the United States—and a flow of words like lava from the volcano of the author's resentment hardens about the notorious inconstancy of all men and events. This, where the cause is admirable, is admirable too, usually commendable, but it is not biography.

Heat, so indispensable to life, is not always a prop to the mind. Indignant men, human volcanoes, are not invariably dependable mentally. Wisdom, it may be, is as impressive as energy. Violence. A cool phrase, like the evening dusk, is very assuring, especially in the description of what, once, was a fact, a fact or a man. The attempted description of a reality must breed confidence if nothing else in the world. Confidence. A belief in the honesty, the clarity and correctness of positive assertions. A biography, even a description of atmosphere, must be positive. It is written for the purposes of explanation and definition. An indignant, a passionately concerned, mind is not honest; truth and causes have little enough in common. A cause may transcend the necessity for truth, sweep forward on lies infinitely nobler than candor, but that is not the business of biographies.

The biography of place or, say, of a political generation, is legitimate but not, strictly, biographical; in it the background is mistaken for the subject. But, then, it is so pleasant, so unlaborious, to write; the preparation, the bibliography, is a delight: works on early transportation, broadhorns and saddle packs and wood-burning locomotives with gilded stacks, early lithographs, maps softly printed from stone, fur trappers' notes, the inexhaustible metal galleries of the Library of Congress. Beautiful material and inexact. The fatality of descriptions, of backgrounds, lies in the fact that for themselves they are worthless. Stupid. Clothes fetched empty from closets of the past. A breath of the picturesque is a poisonous vapor. Quaintness—but it is not necessary to speak of quaintness.

A biography, correctly regarded, is a study of an individual, to the degree that a person can be individual. It is a consideration of uniqueness; and, for that reason, the descriptions of women are very often duller than not. A unique woman is not very engaging; unique, that is, in the performance of singular and objective works. They are usually, such women, lost to the primary object of their being —a certain combination with a masculine individual in the interest of nature. There are, naturally, women who transcend that innocent and primitive plan, but, somewhere in the process of becoming so much, they cease to be women. They are very useful but not profoundly significant. The women of science, women of letters, the feminine masters of mathematics and economics have all, without benefit of choice, paid too dearly for their privileges and learning.

I say that for him.) I heard a little of their private discussion. If they were not ~~confined~~ careful, certain ool said, all they hoped to accomplish would killed on the floor of the Senate."

The conversation, turning to holidays with pay seamen ran last, for Rufus frock, in the evening of Easter troubled on the balcony at the ___-house. He returned to that continually through a sleepless night; it occupied him entering the plenary hall of the International Commission. The hall, for the moment, was filled with an formal confusion; members on the platform and floor were shuffling from ~~center~~ group to group with the mingled accents of a dozen languages; only the Japanese delegation, dark and imperturbable, remained compactly in their seats. ~~This~~ entering the alley Rufus frock encountered Mr. Price. The movement delegate was, patently, disturbed.

"This, now, is called the Reptile House," he joined Rufus, waving toward the assembled and the next wall of glass.) hope it won't prove t

On the other hand, strangely enough, the biographies of women celebrated for their loveliness have been no less unsatisfactory. The business of being a woman is universal and not individual. The truth about one beautiful woman is practically always the truth about the other beautiful creatures—they are vain and cold and self-seeking in their impersonal moments; their more significant, horizontal, encounters cannot be repeatedly described. It is the curious fate of passages devoted to the relations of the sexes to become almost at once unsupportably dull. The common English tradition where love and religion are concerned has no wit, nothing to relieve the sentimental obscenity of its attitude toward them. Love is sacred and religion is sacred. Actually one woman in bed is very much like another woman in bed; her actions, within limits of sincerity and experience and feeling, resemble the actions, identically situated, of all others. Lady Hamilton and Lola Montez, amiable queens and political duchesses, show no emotional variations, no discernible individuality. Not only are they—the diagrammatic facts—dull to regard, but there is, in English, no sufficiently handsome vocabulary for their description. There is—except for scientific words and the colloquial phrases so disastrously employed by D. H. Lawrence and Frank Harris—no vocabulary at all. This, especially in biography, must reduce an indispensable directness, a clarity, of manner to no better than innuendo. Pandering sentences. There is, obviously, a biography of scandal that has its not inconsiderable uses; it is then, however, either irradiated by the detached light of the comic spirit or ironically exhibited as the fatality inseparable from the human heart.

Men are different; not better, perhaps, but different—there are soldiers who are men, statesmen and scientists who are, at the same time, wholly masculine; eminent men, actually, have always been more masculine than normal, commonplace, men. That, it may well be, is the first mark,

[77]

the sign, of their eminence. They appreciated, almost as much as their several remarkable abilities, the charming women who appreciated them. Celebrated men, with the privileges of celebrity, have always exercised their rights in the directions of luxury and pleasure. Why, in the name of God, not! The energy of their accomplishments generated a second, alleviating, power. At the same time it did not interfere with their primary preoccupations—stellar space or the state or patterns of sound.

Richard Wagner, for example, depended to an enormous extent upon the women whose sympathy, and passion, supported his existence, but a proper biography of Wagner is still a work devoted to his genius. The accounts of his love affairs are relatively shabby accomplishments. Chopin has been almost obliterated by the sentimental, and worthless, histories of his life with George Sand. There is, in reality, a serious defect in all men who are slaves to women or a woman, particularly to a woman. They are, sooner or later, smothered in the silken draperies of her couch, the warm and flexible, the debasing, ivory of her body.

Biographies of men, fortunately, must be free from such considerations, except where they are tragic or ideal. The safest woman for a man to hold in his heart is imaginary, a woman seen, remembered, in a veil of unearthly and impossible beauty. Rachel, Andrew Jackson's wife, was like that. The important passages in the life of a soldier take place on the field or in councils of war, and not in the hours of his sensual relaxation; his concern, the burden of his biography, is with war, his military aspirations, his triumphs and failures. I have just finished a biography of General Sheridan, the commander, eventually, of Grant's cavalry, and, reading the proof sheets of pages I had written with enormous difficulty, I was appalled by the coldness of what, within the limitations of my conception, I had produced.

[78]

It was the description, from a great variety and number of sources, of a cavalry general in the Civil War; it was without indignation or a moral, filled with accounts of battles, the advancing and ebbing tides of war; and I wondered how, in the partisan heat and colored clamor of biography today, I could hope for any success.

There was, in any consideration of General Sheridan, an especial difficulty created by the wide difference between his solid accomplishments and great public acclaim. His reputation, actually, was made by a set of indifferent verses. Indifferent and inaccurate. Sheridan was an able officer, his good luck was remarkable, but his ability, at bottom, was the reverse of spectacular: his popularity and success with soldiers lay in the fact that he took splendid care of them. General Sheridan's beginning experience with the Civil War he adorned was in the Quartermaster's department; he had to do with the movement of supplies to the front. Consequently later he had a sharp eye to the comfort of his troops; they were well fed and their camps were as sanitary as it was possible to make them. The romantic tradition established by the Confederate cavalry leaders was, after the war, extended to include General Sheridan; but he had no right to it; what he did possess, however, was more valuable—he was a practical and fortunate commander. And it was, therefore, necessary to establish my biography of General Sheridan in the face of a universal, a different and infinitely more glamorous, tradition.

The element of persistent good fortune that followed him was, in a literal work, even more difficult to deal with. His first promotion to the rank of general officer was the reward of brilliant fighting and steadiness at Booneville and Stone's River, but his subsequent fame, if not his actual rise, was founded upon chance: his charge up Missionary Ridge was no more than the result of a mistake made by Grant. Sheridan had been manoeuvred into an untenable position. His even more celebrated ride from Winchester to the front at Cedar Creek, in the Great Valley of Virginia—there are a number of conflicting accounts about that—was, plainly viewed, made necessary by his neglect to rejoin the armies of the Shenandoah with sufficient promptness after a consultation with Mr. Seward and the President in Washington, October 17, 1864. He stayed, the truth is, two nights on the way from Martinsburg to Cedar Creek, a distance slightly under forty miles.

What engaged him is not wholly problematic—a general agreement of rumor and local, immediate, memories, anonymous but convincing, asserts that he was pleasantly employed with drink. Probably. I was, however, more interested in the result of his delay than by its cause. That, it seemed to me, in a military biography, was sufficiently indicated by a bare statement. It resulted, certainly, in uselessly sacrificing hundreds of lives, but for General Sheridan it was a way to a vastly greater fame. It was not part of my undertaking to comment upon anything, but only to repeat, as far as it was possible, what actually had occurred. I had no impulse, no need, to uphold or excuse General Sheridan; I owned, in reality, no particular enthusiasm for him as a human being; he was a notable commander of cavalry.

For those reasons I brought my biography to an end with the end of the Civil War; Sheridan became involved with the politics of Reconstruction, in Louisiana, and, outside the field of battle, he was honest but insignificant. I put what, generally, happened to him before the Rebellion into a single chapter, and dispensed, as far as it could be managed, with atmosphere. No one, I informed myself, outside a few retired, and contentious, army officers and some impatient historians, would read my careful narrative of battles and marches. I regretted that, but chiefly on account of Ferris Greenslet, who had suggested a biography of General Sheridan to me. That, it seemed to me, was a compliment; I had hoped that his firm, Houghton Mifflin Company, would recover their expenses in my undertaking and perhaps a little more. But I was determined not to change the form of my conception to make a fortune for anyone. I regarded the biography of General Sheridan in the light of a luxury, a work that would ignore everything but the integrity of its design, the requirements, in other words, of my pride.

The preliminary bibliographical study I accomplished in Washington, at the Carlton Hotel, with the assistance of a radio and the Library of Congress. Except for occasional lunches with Laura Curtis it was neither easy nor pleasant. The detailed histories of battles are commonly dry and, more often than not, partisan. Undependable. The topography of the battles around Chattanooga was, practically, impossible to describe, a confusion of mountains and valleys and coves, of creeks and rivers. I wanted to make it clear to the mind, to show where and how the armies of the North faced the Southern army. Sheridan's exact situations. There were, on different maps, different names for the same places. The problem of style, of clarity, harassed me—the number of commanders, for example, Federal and Confederate, named Smith involved in one paragraph.

It became clear, as I progressed, that General Sheridan had been subjected to some very awkward criticism. He had not, in Tennessee, except at Missionary Ridge, covered himself with anything resembling glory. Later, in the Shenandoah Valley, he became rather celebrated for his retreats before Jubal Early's inferior numbers. But that was more in his favor than not—he was a practical, a professional, soldier. At the same time it made him difficult to explain in martial and ringing phrases. I would, I saw at once, have to give them up. Politics, operating little if at all with Sheridan, was still an important part of the battles he engaged in: the stupidity of General Halleck, Mr. Lin-

coln's Chief of Staff, the curiously involved, the frigid and
self-seeking, character of Mr. Seward. I had to become
familiar with the deliberations in Washington and the jeal-
ousies on the field. It was all the reverse of stirring or romantic. The Civil War, I had thought, was a romantic
war; I had already written a measurably romantic book
about it; but, studied closely, the appearance of romance,
at least in my consideration of General Sheridan, evaporated.

I had to become familiar with the European ambitions
and desperate hopes of the Confederacy, and learn the economics of cotton; I was forced to follow to their futile ends
all the efforts at a premature peace, to analyse Horace
Greeley's ill-tempered relationship with the Administra-
tion. I wished twenty times in a day that I had never heard
of General Sheridan. Shut in my rooms at the Carlton
Hotel, with a table full of Civil War accounts and authorities, I came to hate him and the biography of him I had so
lightly agreed to write. Later, at Palm Beach, actually engaged upon it, my hatred increased; I wrote, when it was
humanly possible, three thousand words a day, and often
it took an hour to put down a line, a word. My mind, it
seemed to me, froze.

I left the cursed book, the bitch of a biography, and
fished in the Gulf Stream for sailfish; but all the while,
swinging over the glassy indigo ground swell, I was pre-
occupied and worried by General Sheridan. I returned to
Washington, proceeded to West Chester, with my undertaking unfinished; and then, in a vast energy, I brought it
to a close. I finished it and read, and corrected, two sets of
proofs, concerned with properly designating literally hundreds of regiments, hundreds of officers, hundreds of obscure locations. Even that, finally, came to an end. The
biography of General Sheridan was almost completely
what I had planned, but almost no one, I repeated to myself, would buy it. A book empty of ornament and of sup-

porting, reassuring, illusion. Fired by no passion, dignified by no cause, whatever. The biography of General Philip H. Sheridan in the Civil War. But I thought of it, at last, with affection. I was glad that it was what it was. For myself. That, after all, was the hidden reward of reputable accomplishment.

ROBINSON JEFFERS

Born Pittsburgh, Pennsylvania, January 10, 1887.
Attended private schools in Switzerland and Germany.
A.B., Occidental College, 1905. Postgraduate work abroad.
Married. Author: *Californians* (1916), *Descent to the Dead*
(1931), *Solstice and Other Poems* (1935). Home: Carmel,
California.

FIRST BOOK appeared in Part Ten of The Colophon;
May, 1932.

> *Tor House, Carmel, Calif.*
> *January 11, 1937*

Dear Mr. Adler:

    Thank you for your letter re *"Getting Into Print." I
am sorry not to have answered more promptly, and hope this is not
too late for your purpose.*

    *My book-manuscript is written in pencil and typed by
myself; no one else could read it. Almost all changes and revisions
are made in the pencil draft, very few in the process of typing, none
later. I usually see one set of proofs and hate it.*

    *Enclosed is a quite characteristic page from the un-
finished manuscript of my next book. I'm afraid it is too dim and
queer for reproduction, but that is in the nature of my handwriting.*

    Cordially yours,

        Robinson Jeffers

the eagles nest on the _____ of an east rock released, my own

of the precipice — fretted ridges
Mount Verdure — broad, the _____ craggy wild
1/5/ed country a _____ mostly but
_____
hills _____ house plains; our _____
_____ those _____ hunting _____ its mighty
_____

_____ _____ _____ _____
hight the knighed ones?
_____

the nest is _____ and it
one _____ wide stile the will

_____ features to these fortress.
The she-eagle of war, to make her short-long go, she
is never _____ with a sea of home.

who lightning blasted her and she _____ it _____ in
the same _____ in the splendid the _____ in the
the _____ fires O; she _____

The she-eagle is older than O, stored in these ridges,

Robinson Jeffers

I AM WILLING to tell the history of my first book, though it is not clear why it should interest anyone; certainly it does not interest me. In 1912 I came into possession of a little money, a little more than was immediately required, a novel experience. I had written verses, like almost everybody, and had not offered them to magazines, but it occurred to me that now I could afford to get them printed. For the purpose I made acquaintance with an older author of verses who was somehow interested in a printing-shop called the Grafton Publishing Company. I asked him to luncheon, drank with him, and showed him my typewritten little poems. I believe he really thought well of them, although it seems to me now an impossible generosity. It was arranged that they should be made into a book; I was very willing to pay for the manufacture of five hundred copies, and took away my manuscript to arrange it for the printer.

This was in Los Angeles; I lived rather solitary at one of the beaches twenty miles distant, and was too young for my age, and drank a good deal when I came up to town. At Redondo, on my way home in the evening, I left the electric car to visit a bar-room frequented by longshoreman friends of mine. I stayed there until the cars stopped running, and had to walk the three miles home. For several hours I had thought nothing about my verses, which only interested part of my mind, for I had no confidence in them. It was not until the next morning that I looked for the bundle of manuscript; which had been under my arm, but it must have been laid down somewhere, and was not to be found, either at home or in Redondo. The loss was not serious in any sense; not even serious for the moment, because I have always had an excellent memory for trifles, and every line and rhyme was lodged in my head, only needing to be typewritten again.

A name had to be found for the book, and discovering that all the verses were more or less amatory, I thought sadly of the conversation reported in George Moore's *Confessions of a Young Man*, which I had lately read. "My dear Dayne, you always write about love; the subject is nauseating."—"So it is; but after all Baudelaire wrote about love and lovers; his best poem—"—"True, *mais il s'agissait d'une charogne*—there was a carrion in it, and that elevates the tone considerably." But I had no *charogne* in my little verses, and was never witty, and could only think of the line in the Song of Songs, "Stay me with flagons, comfort me with apples, for I am sick of love." So the small book was called *Flagons and Apples*, a title much too big for it.

Something was said at the printing-shop about sending out review copies; but my interest in the book was waning, the irrational need of publication seemed to be satisfied by the printing, and nothing further was done.

Soon after this, life became more interesting than anybody's book; I went away to Seattle and left my 480 volumes in the printer's cellar. Twenty I had taken; I gave away three or four, and later burned the rest. I cannot remember how much time passed before a letter from the printer reached me in Seattle, asking what he should do with the volumes left on his hands. I told him to have them pulped, I remember thinking that perhaps their substance would save a young forest-tree from the paper mills. But the honest printer wanted to cut my loss; he sold the whole edition to a second-hand book-shop, for twenty cents

A·B·C·D·E·F·G·H·I·K·L·M·R·J·N·O·P·Q·S·T·U·V·W·X·Y·Z

apiece, I cannot imagine how it was accomplished, and sent me the check. Holmes's Book-store—or was it Dawson's?—remained of course unable to re-sell their bargain; I have lately heard that they were reduced to giving away the volumes, and would broadcast them to be scrambled for, at auctions of other books.

I had had my printing and was satisfied for four years, until a new accumulation of verses began to trouble me. This time I thought of regular publication, and mailed my manuscript across the continent to the Macmillan Company, who astonished me with a favorable answer. This book was called *Californians*; it found no readers, but it seems interesting that it found an excellent publisher at the first attempt. After this I wrote many verses but was entirely unable to get them published, and I am glad of that.

In 1920 or 1921 I wrote a story in verse called *Tamar*; and I have heard that it was sent in vain to publisher after publisher, but that is not true. It was offered to none; it was so lengthy that I believed no publisher's reader would look through it. *Tamar* was kept in a drawer until I saw a little advertisement by a New York printer, Peter G. Boyle, in a book-review section of *The New York Times*. Boyle has since then retired from his business. The advertisement offered printing, not publishing, and my mind reverted to my folly of 1912, yet with differences. This time I had no extra money burning my pocket; on the other hand, it seemed to me that the verses were not merely negligible, like the old ones, but had some singularity, whether they were good or not. Perhaps, if they were printed, someone might look at them sometime—*habent sua fata libelli*—little books have such queer destinies. Boyle read *Tamar and Other Poems*, and set a price on the printing, one that I knew was very moderate. He added some praise of *Tamar* that seemed to me excessive, but I learned later that he was sincerely enthusiastic about it. After several months of hesitation I

[89]

told him to print, but only five hundred copies, not the thousand that he advised.

Publishing was not in the bargain, but Peter Boyle was generous, and did his utmost as a publisher. He sent review copies in all directions, at his own expense of time and postage; but quite in vain, no one would notice the book. Suddenly he despaired, and shipped me 450 copies in a big packing-box, across the continent. I stowed them under the eaves in the attic.

Meanwhile, the Book Club of California was preparing an anthology of verse by California writers, afterwards called *Continent's End*. George Sterling, James Rorty and Genevieve Taggard were the editors. Someone, having perhaps heard of my Macmillan volume, told them that I also wrote verses; and a letter came from Rorty asking me to contribute. I sent some pages of verse; and when *Tamar* was printed I mailed a copy to Rorty because of our correspondence, and one to George Sterling because he had lived in Carmel before my time, and knew the scene of my stories.

Rorty was only temporarily in California; when he returned to the East he persuaded Mark Van Doren to read *Tamar*. Soon a review of the book by Rorty appeared in the Herald-Tribune *Books*, Mark Van Doren wrote about it in the *Nation*, and Babette Deutsch in the *New Republic*.

I received a telegram from Peter Boyle saying that people wanted to buy *Tamar* and he had none to sell; then the big packing-box, as big as a coffin, was dragged out from under the eaves and shipped back to New York. As it emptied, Boyle proposed to print a second edition, but on second thought he decided that a more established publisher might be to my advantage. He offered the book to Boni and Liveright, and it was reprinted in my *Roan Stallion* volume. It pleases me to think of Boyle's honesty and good will, and of the active generosity of Rorty, Mark Van

Doren, George Sterling and some others, to a writer at that time perfectly unknown to them.

To close the story, it appears that the Los Angeles book-shop which so recklessly bought the edition of *Flagons and Apples* had not been able to dispose of it, even by giving it away at auctions. There were still copies in the cellar; after *Tamar* was spoken of they were dug out and sold for more than they had cost. So now it has become impossible for me to buy them up and drown them, as I should like to.

MacKINLAY KANTOR

Born Webster City, Iowa, February 4, 1904.
Educated high schools of Webster City and of Des Moines
and Chicago. Worked as newspaper reporter, advertising
man, free-lance writer, scenario writer. Married. Author:
Long Remember (1934), *The Voice of Bugle Ann* (1935), *Arouse
and Beware* (1936). Home: Westfield, New Jersey.

MY MEMOIRS OF THE CIVIL WAR appeared in
Volume One, Number Four, new series The Colophon;
June, 1936.

Sarasota, Florida
February 2, 1937

My Dear Adler:

I hope this is what you want.

With kindest regards,

Mack K

*1. Do you (a) first write out your notes by hand, or (b)
do you work directly on a typewriter?*

*As soon as I began to write (when I was about sixteen
or seventeen years old), I wrote all prose directly on the typewriter.
I suppose this was because I grew up, more or less, in a small-
town newspaper office. Verse was written in longhand with pencil,
and, as is usually the case with young poets, on any paper available.*

I remember when I was about twenty-one, how I got a severe emotional wallop out of leaving my work as rodman with a surveying party, begging some brown wrapping paper from the proprietor of a roadside hot-dog stand, and sitting down to write my poem with surveyor's crayon and with the paper held securely on the flat side of a surveyor's stick. It was one of those silly conceits very satisfying when you are twenty-one.

A year ago last December I began for the first time to dictate. I was sure that it would be almost impossible for me to do this, but thought it worth a try. I had excellent success with magazine short stories from the start, which encouraged me to try a novel a few months later. That was Arouse and Beware. *With the exception of a very few brief scenes, it was written between April and September 1936, and was dictated entirely.*

2. Also, (a) is your copy retyped by yourself for sending on to the publisher, or (b) is it typed by someone else?

I dictate to my secretary perhaps 1500 or 2000 words, or even more, at a stretch. She takes it down in shorthand and transcribes it, double space, on the typewriter. The following day or night, usually, I read this copy carefully and make many penciled deletions and corrections. Then I put that copy aside to cool and go on with fresh dictation. I am apt to have anywhere from five to twenty-five thousand words "cooling" at a single time. This copy is read by me a second, third, fourth, and perhaps a fifth time with more penciled corrections or substitutions at each reading—until the original, double-spaced manuscript is a horrid sight to behold.

When I have decided that it is ready to go, I give it to Miss Rankin and she types it, including all the changes marked, and making two carbons. This final copy I usually read a couple of times before giving it to my publisher; if possible, I read it aloud to long-suffering relatives and friends. I watch their reactions closely, and if I consider a kick justified, I try to make amends. In all, I suppose I read each part of the novel at least twelve or fifteen times before it is published, and by that time I am so sick of it that I cannot strenuously object to what the most vituperative critic has to say. It appears flat and dull and sickening to me, and I wonder seriously just why Timmy Coward should want to take the rap.

3. Of course, if you dictate the original copy we should like very much to know that.

Answered above.

4. After your copy is set in type are you in the habit of receiving more than one proof—that is, any additional revised proofs?

I read as many proofs as possible: galleys, revised galleys if there is time, and pages. My secretary reads them also, checking carefully with the original manuscript. The revised page proof we check only with the previous proof, in order to see that the proper corrections have been made.

5. And do you make any changes in your copy after it is set in type?

On the whole, I think we make very few changes after the copy is once set in type. Of course, the time element entered into it strongly in the case of Arouse and Beware; *we were up against a deadline, and a number of typographical errors got into the first edition.*

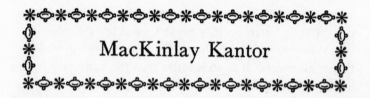

MacKinlay Kantor

IF I HAD BEEN born thirty-eight years and ten months sooner, I would have been born during the week when the Army of Northern Virginia crept west from Petersburg to silence its last pathetic snarlings at Appomattox. But I was born in 1904, and historians of the future may declare that the generation born in 1904 did not know the taste of the Rebellion.

Until I live to hear them make that assertion, I cannot argue with them. It is my belief, however, that we of 1904 (at least those of us who grew into the towns which still had something of their pioneer youth and rawness) were far closer to the War between the States—far closer than the generation of 1956, now lying unrealized within the bodies of children at nursery school, will ever be to the Great War with Germany.

For, day by day, we have lost the threads that tied us to an America long shadowed by the wings of passenger pigeons. Thirty years ago there were hot campfires in the parlors of midwestern homes, ready to melt the past decades into a common wax for the asking. And when the Fords and Chevrolets came, and Douglas Fairbanks and William S. Hart and Theda Bara came, and when the town jeweler set up an aerial for wireless telegraphy on the roof of his store, and snared the SOS call of a ship in trouble off Havana; and, after that, when the generations of 1898 and

1900 went yelling away to Camp Dodge, and the generation of 1904 hated itself because it couldn't follow—

When all of those things happened, and the crueler
things afterward, it is no wonder that the campfires in the
little parlors went out. I venture no prophecy about the
date of their re-kindling, and I feel sorry for the babies of
1956.

Because I was born into a bold illusion, authentic and
sententious, like the basso profundo of drums in front of the
G.A.R. hall. The keepers of this illusion lived in nearly
every house, and while some few of them were as frail and
querulous and papery as the patriarchs whom I met in
Grand Rapids last September, many were young enough
to take part in the fat men's race at the county fair, or to
engage in a Saturday night fist-fight behind the Park Hotel.

My grandmother had married at sixteen, and so, although the grandfather in our house could remember well
enough how the blue-freighted packets looked, sailing
downstream from Dubuque, he was too young to have been
a passenger on one of them. The Civil War lived in Grand-
ma's button-bag, and it was my great-grandfather who had
put it there. On rainy Sunday afternoons I used to take the
Civil War out of the button-bag and play with it on the
floor. There were the large, brass buttons which had fastened Grandpa Bone's blouse down the front, and the
smaller ones which had adorned his sleeves. There was a
shoulder-strap, too, with its single bars of stiff, gold braid;
and upstairs we had a picture of him which would have ter-
rified me if I had not known that, in spite of his angry eyes,
he was an old soldier. And all old soldiers were kind to little
boys.

Of course, there was the Waldron place across the river
where we dared not go for walnuts because old Fritz Waldron would come after us with a cattle whip; and there were
old Herrington, who swore under his whiskey breath whenever the boys tagged him at his lawn-mowing work, and

Dr. Sill, who would stop his buggy and threaten to call the marshal if a boy caught on behind. But in spite of these glaring and dangerous exceptions to the rule, we were all nursed in the belief that every old soldier worthy of the name was a man of genial and courageous parts, schooled in adherence to the Apostles' Creed, the Emancipation Proclamation, and "A Visit from St. Nicholas." And so help me, if ever paragon lived to support a common mis-apprehension, at least a dozen such paragons lived in the Webster City, Iowa, of the early nineteen-hundreds. Astride their graves, I will challenge posterity to deny it.

Thus far I have offered no adequate explanation for a personal fixation on the Civil War, and have cited no experience or acquaintance which could not be considered common to that age and place. Perhaps I was enlisted in the Civil War from birth, first, by the persistent sentimentality of the grandmother in whose home I lived, and, second, by the influence of a younger woman who had transmuted that earnest sentimentality into a fervent, scholarly interest in Americana of the Mississippi Valley.

She was my mother, and during the years which have passed since she left me, I find my debt compounding each week at an interest-rate which will bankrupt me unless I work harder than I have worked before. She covered our walls with pictures of bison, and battles, and log court-houses, and mill-stones. She weighed down the table in the living room with well-rubbed books, and stuffed the corners of the old secretary with yellow newspaper clippings.

From the time I could walk as far as the hill beyond the creek valley, the Sundays of my memory glitter and hum . . . we were gone by ten o'clock in the morning, we excused ourselves from the requisite church of Iowa, and I drank my first and happiest coffee from a black tin pail in Hamilton County's pastures and wood lots. Here was the old Chase mill dam, here was the mysterious brick house that Ulis Briggs had built in the middle of an oak forest,

here was a high, gaunt strip of prairie where Sidominadotah
had ridden with his Sioux.

The survivors of the Spirit Lake Massacre relief ex-
pedition and the Northern Border Brigade, came to our
house: stooped, bony old men with deep eyes and opin-
ionated jaws, and tongues ready to gossip for hours on end.
Amid their nasal reminiscences, I heard again the swift
scream of fifes which had sounded to me when I was three
years old and played with the button-bag.

Across a wide yard, and on a hillside beyond our house,
lived a ne'er-do-well teamster who was my first great love,
and who was possessed by that charity of spirit which nature
uses sometimes as sorry compensation for incompetence
in a preying world. But not the least of Mr. McFarland's
gifts to me was his father-in-law, Grandpa Wicks, an
elderly cabinet-maker who carried memories of the Twenty-
ninth Wisconsin Volunteer Infantry along with him in his
tool satchel. Once Grandpa Wicks had been wounded—
that was a few days before the surgeons made a one-armed
carpenter out of him—and he lay for hours in the full tor-
ment of a Confederate sun. As in a thousand Civil War
tales, so alike as to be almost Biblical in their ubiquity,
Grandpa Wicks was befriended by a dying rebel, who
poured down his throat the traditional measure of cold
water.

The water was poured from a canteen; I was five years
old when I heard this, and the metallic suggestion of the
word canteen rang in my ears for hours. Canteen . . . I had
heard the lusty or cracked voices at the courthouse park a
few weeks before, when the old guard of Hamilton County
met in reunion.

> *We have drank from the same canteen, boys,*
> *We have drank from the same canteen.*

The nearest that I could come to it, at long last, was a
tin can; I found one on top of the refrigerator, an empty

A·B·C·D·E·F·G·H·I·J·L·N·M·K·O·P·Q·R·S·T·U·V·W·X·Y·Z

coffee can. Canteen, can tin, tin can. I filled it at the pump
and carried it with me to the hill above the corn-field that
fell away below our barn. Spread-eagled flat against the
blue-grass, I lay there with eyes closed until the sun seemed
ready to shrivel the lids apart; and I was Grandpa Wicks
for a while, and in the end I was a rebel, dying; and I
poured the water slowly down my parched throat out of
my tin can canteen.

That was how I suffered my first wound in the Civil
War, though many were to come later—nearly twenty-five
years later, in fact, when I wore out my eyes building up
the necessary historical background for *Long Remember*. And
in contemplating those wounds, I am as full of self-satisfac-
tion—selfish, petulant, childish pride—as any hollow-
cheeked relic who lingers, rocking on the porch of a Soldiers' Home and denying shrilly that Grover Cleveland
ever cut the soldiers' pensions.

And then there were John Kearns, who let me hold in
my hand the ounce ball which had splintered into his
femur at Vicksburg, and Park Banks, so slim and trim and
dapper that he looked more at home squiring pretty school-
marms to the Knights Templar banquets than he did
marching with the other veterans on Decoration Day.
Close in the squad behind them strode Bob White, whose
rank exalted itself in his aging mind until, at his death, he
was convinced that he had commanded a brigade; and old
Mr. Jacks with a face like an Indian; and the Hon. Wesley
Martin, superintendent of our Sunday School, who stood
pointing his nose-glasses at us every Sunday before May
30th, year in and year out, declaring, "And the first time
I lifted a musket to my shoulder I do not believe that I hit
the state of Virginia, although I was right in the middle of
it!" I am grateful to them for whatever heroic marches they
may have made, but more than that, for whatever truths
or lies any one of them may have told.

... There came a young man in a seersucker suit, who

[101]

sat fanning himself in our living room, and explaining rapidly to my grandmother that she should buy *The Photographic History of the Civil War*, complete in ten volumes, edited by Francis Trevelyan Miller and published by the Review of Reviews Company.

Even in the McKinlay household, coal for the kitchen range was more necessary than the brave stand of Major-General George H. Thomas, and Mr. Scriven's grocery bill leaped automatically to a position surmounting that of the battle of Resaca. There wasn't much money in the old tooth-pick holder on the clock shelf, and not much more in the bank, and the grain-buying business didn't seem to prosper in the hands of my grandfather.

The young man in the seersucker suit had a vast sheaf of photographs, loose-leaf pages or proofs, carried with him for purposes of demonstration. I like to think that he took heart wholly because of the earnest pleading with which I importuned my grandmother. "Anyway," he said, "I will leave these pictures here for a day or two, and you folks can glance through them. Madam, I am quite confident that by the time I come back you will have been convinced that you cannot afford to let the members of your household be without this beautiful set of books, bound appropriately in blue cloth, and stamped in gold."

After he was gone, I spread the pictures on the floor, and I do not think I got up until supper-time. And some kind of god, perhaps the same god who is alleged to be kind to dogs and old soldiers and newsboys, did appear unto that young man in a dream and tell him to go him into all the world and preach the gospel of *The Photographic History of the Civil War* to every creature. At any rate, he didn't come back. If our house had ever caught fire, and I had been there, those loose-leaved proofs would have been the first thing carried out.

And then it was late May again, and all the buggies and Ramblers and Overlands and Marions lined up along

was (symbolically pried) from the foundations of the old North

Building; —another year would see its scoty turrets and rat-

tling — windows — by — contractors--another

thirteen months would see the — wires strung around the a

fresh-rolled excavation where the sour-smelling cellars had been)

and where — piteous blades of newly germinated

grass — would struggle to grow.

— muscular fingers on

the window sill, and wondered about the principalship of the new

Junior High School.

Seventh, eighth, and ninth grades, — it was rumored that the salary of a

practical instructor

principal, might run as high as $175.00 a month. No

one as yet had made official mention, or even unofficial offer

to Fitch, and there would be girls in the Junior High School--more

girls than boys, of course--and Fitch had never taught girls.

Prospect street—Prospect street, that began at a coal yard along the Illinois Central tracks, and ended at the cemetery. Here marched the Webster City band in the fullest spirit of its brass, and here rode Press Hyatt, ordinarily the plump proprietor of the Orpheum moving picture theater, but on this day swollen to even mightier proportions as the colonel of the Fifty-sixth Iowa Militia. And here came the I.N.G.'s, and George Yaus with his bugle, and the ladies of the W.R.C., and a plethora of flags. And here marched, also, the old soldiers, and there were a good company of them in that year. Ahead of them, skirling, squealing, booming like a battery of three-inch rifles, staggered the drum corps.

I was ready for this music, now, although I had not known it before. I trotted alongside the drum corps, and pattered through the dust of the cemetery lane and in through the wide gate. When the last volley of the firing squad had sounded, I lit out for home; I acquainted my lips frantically, over and over, with the song which the drum corps had played—a song born in the stubborn, cocksure spirit of the American eighteenth century.

It was played at Monmouth and Lundy's Lane and Chapultepec, and ten million times in the Civil War. It is still played wherever there is one rheumy, creaking relic to be transported in a parade. Everyone knows the tune. Everyone says, "What? Oh, yes. I know. It's the song the old soldiers always play." And yet one American in a thousand, or perhaps in ten thousand, can tell you the name. Originally, I believe it was known as "Paul Revere's Ride," and down east there are old men who declare it to be "The Gobby O." And every member of the National Association of Civil War Musicians insists that the correct title is "Jefferson and Liberty."

I whistled it all the way down the hill and along Ohio street, and past the cedars in front of the old Martin place. I whistled it across the yard and into our own dining room.

My grandmother came quickly from the kitchen, with a dish cloth in her hands. Her eyes were very bright. "Honey," she said, "that tune . . . I never heard you whistle that before. It sounds like—"

I cried, "It's a swell tune! The old soldiers just played it up at the cemetery—old man Lee, and Dr. Homan, and everybody. Here's how it goes," and I shrieked the thing once more, until the cat ran and hid under the sofa.

My grandmother began to cry. "Pa used to play that," she said. And that was the first I knew that my great-grandfather, too, had been a Civil War musician.

ROCKWELL KENT

Born Tarrytown Heights, New York, June 21, 1882.
Educated at Horace Mann School, New York, and Columbia University. Studied art. Married. Has exhibited
widely, and is represented in many American galleries.
Author *Wilderness* (1920), *N by E* (1930), *Salamina* (1935),
etc. Home: Ausable Forks, New York.

ALIAS KENT, BY HOGARTH, JR. appeared in
Part Thirteen of The Colophon; February, 1933.

Ausable Forks, N. Y.
March 28, 1937

Dear Mr. Adler:

*A few days ago, after I had finished a lecture and was
trying to make a quick get-away, a lady collared me and said, with
what seemed to me a good deal of indignation, "Mr. Kent, you
contradicted yourself in your lecture." "Well," I said getting into
my coat, "you have the advantage of me in this discussion. You
heard the lecture and I didn't."*

*I know that I have written books because there they are
elegantly bound on my shelves. But just how I do it I can't quite
remember. I suspect that my wife has a great deal to do with the
matter because my manuscript, handwritten in a script so small that
I can't read it myself without a reading glass, and scrawled over,*

scratched out, re-written, annotated, interlarded so that almost no one else could read it even with a telescope, is actually deciphered and typed by my wife who, if she can't make out what I've written, knows me well enough to know what I'd like to have written. The result from her hand is what my publisher sees.

I don't write out notes. The first word is the seed from which all the rest eventually grows. I write two or three lines and then I read them aloud. Then I light a cigarette, walk up and down awhile, sit down, and scratch out what I've written. Then I try it again. The manuscript of Salamina is about six times as long as the final book.

I make lots of changes in the copy after it has been set in type. The changes that I make are practically all restorations of the original errors in punctuation and sentence structure that the well-trained publisher's proofreader couldn't let go by. Then I have to be on my guard against such meticulous craftsmen in printing as, dear Elmer, yourself. I call to your mind your recent suggestion that you change the words in a sentence of mine so that the type would come out even at the end of a line.

I think that's all.

Faithfully yours,

Rockwell Kent

THE ancient class of 1904, Architecture Columbia, was housed on the top floor of the Havemeyer Building. There, remote from college life, we sat on high stools bent over our drawing boards grinding out projects of Roman baths and stadiums, while our brothers of the Arts and Sciences disported, if it pleased them to, in the swimming pool and on the track of the University. We were a group apart, unknown to our fellow classmates.

There was among us a young fellow named Marcus, who had so quaint a sense of his own importance that it became our pleasure, if not our need, to put him from time to time upside down in a huge waste paper hamper that had been, seemingly, contrived for just that use.

It is the time-honored custom at Columbia for every class during its Junior year to publish a memorial book of the personnel and activities of the class; and, among the many honors that are at the bestowal of the undergraduates, membership on that board of editors ranks high. The board was chosen by election at a general meeting of the class, and it consisted as a rule of men distinguished for their strength, good looks and popularity. We architects were out of it.

The time for the election of our board had come. Two hours before the meeting Marcus struggled out of the waste paper basket, reflected for a moment, and then coming straight to my table addressed me as follows:

"Say: how would you like to be an editor on the *Columbian* board?"

"Fine!" I said. "But no architect stands a chance."

"You leave that to me," said Marcus; he was always cocksure. "And how about another man? How about Squires?"

THE CONDUCTOR

Puck

Now Squires was a gifted post-graduate from Williams. He had been a great pole vaulter, gymnast, all-round trackman and hockey player; he was my elder, my superior in sport and my equal in genius.

"Grand!" I said. The plan amused me.

"Well," said Marcus, "the meeting is at twelve thirty. Meet me at the door downstairs at twelve."

A·B·C·D·E·F·G·H·I·J·L·M·R·K·N·O·P·Q·S·T·U·V·W·X·Y·Z

And at that hour Squires and I were there. Marcus and two friends were waiting for us.

"Shake hands," said Marcus, "with Mr. Tannenbaum and Mr. Katz."

ARCHITEC‑TONICS
The Tales of

TomThumtack
Architect
Volume One

The William T. Comstock Company
New York
MCMXIV.

"Be at the meeting," said Mr. Tannenbaum, and the three of them left us.

The meeting was packed; and among the hundreds of men of the Sciences and Arts the little group of architects on hand was lost. The Chairman rose, made a few polished, pertinent remarks and called for nominations. Names were called out. Smith—Jones—Brown—Robinson; among them I heard ours. The chairman wrote the names on the blackboard, all but mine and Squires'. At that omission it was as though the whole assemblage rose and roared our names. "Who are they?" I heard men round me say. It was a bit

PLUTARCH LIGHTS OF HISTORY
Harper's Weekly

embarrassing. When the list of nominees had been completed ballots were passed around. Each voter wrote a name, folded his slip and passed it to the platform. The electors counted votes. At last the Chairman rose, turned to the blackboard and wrote down results. I was first, then Squires; and the rest were nowhere.

Squires and I as specialists in art persuaded the board to make an art committee of us, with, as a third member,

[110]

one Jack Knox, the artist pride of the Arts. We made me chairman. We divided the pictorial work of the Annual into three lots, assigning one part to each of us. The entire horrible art work was finally turned out by an art mill of some two or three of us. That was my first job as illustrator; —and my last for years. Thus shamefully was Hogarth, Jr., procreated.

THE COMMUTER
Vanity Fair

One day years later when I was working as a draughts-man for the firm of Ewing and Chappell, Architects, Fred Squires walked in to see me.

"I have written a book," he said. "Short stories about architecture, and I want you to illustrate it. I get a hundred dollars for the book and you get a hundred dollars for the pictures."

"Wonderful!" I said. "Let's start."

[111]

So, working at night with Squires at my elbow prompting me and keeping me awake and bringing down the axe when in his judgment what I had done would do, we did those drawings. Dozens of them. So the book was published: *Architectonics*, by Tom Thumtack. Some of the drawings are good, some medium and some worthless, but

THE TALKER
Life

they mark the beginning of that style which, if anything did, distinguished the later work of Hogarth, Jr. It shows him in his adolescence.

More years now passed, and still I found myself working over the drawing boards of Ewing and Chappell; and nobody, draughtsman or boss, was making much out of it. If houses were being built, we weren't designing them, and that is hard to understand, for rarely can there have been assembled in the confines of one small architect's establishment as much genius as George Chappell, poet, and potential Hogarth, Jr., embodied.

CHARLIE CHAPLIN

"Let's try combining poetry and art," said George, and he gave me a creation of his called, I think "The Avenue." I made a picture of the Avenue with all the ardor that the lines inspired, and with the poem and the picture went to the offices of *Vanity Fair*.

Harper's Weekly

"Splendid!" said Frank Crowninshield. "Charming! Delightful! My boy, you have real talent! But," he said, looking at the drawing, "this isn't signed!"

[113]

A·B·C·D·E·F·G·H·I·J·L·M·R·K·N·O·P·Q·S·T·U·V·W·X·Y·Z

"I know it," I said, getting terribly embarrassed. "I don't like to sign it."

"Oh, but we must have a name. Give yourself a name. How about Young Landseer?"

"No, no!" I cried, "Not that, if you please, sir. How about—" and I picked a name at random—"William Hogarth, Jr.?" Thus was I christened.

So it went on for a long time, for a great many years, that combination of poetry and art, George Chappell and Hogarth, Jr. We didn't make much, ten or fifteen dollars apiece at the beginning, but it freed us both from dependence on architecture. I remember being commissioned to make a drawing of Sherry's at the lunch hour. I had never been to Sherry's and to see it at the lunch hour I would have to eat there. I knew it would cost more, to take a guest, than I could get for the drawing. I went alone. The drawing occupied almost a full page in *Vanity Fair;* it was accompanied by George Chappell's verses. The drawing was held to be so splendid an achievement that I was asked to allow *Vanity Fair* to present the original to Mr. Sherry. I think I netted three dollars and twenty-five cents on the whole transaction.

Frank Crowninshield was my steady patron for years. I would visit him regularly with a portfolio of my products and generally dispose of some to him. I showed him once a drawing that I liked particularly. He looked at it, expressed no interest, and returned it to me. I took the drawing home, put a mat around it, drew some elegant lines on the mat making it look like what is called a French mat, wrapped it in tissue paper, protected it with heavy boards and tied it up in the perfection of style and neatness. I went to him two weeks later with the package.

"I dropped in merely in passing, Mr. Crowninshield, to show you something that I am quite proud of." And, clearing the table in front of me, I unwrapped and revealed the drawing. Mr. Crowninshield was fairly staggered by its beauty. He is a gifted appreciator and set me blushing to the roots of my hair with what he told me.

"I don't suppose," he said at last, "that you would consider for a moment permitting us to use this drawing."

I reflected. Then—"Yes, Mr. Crowninshield, I will."

So by this little manner of doing things I won not only praise but a bigger check than I had ever had.

ROLLO IN SOCIETY

Perhaps the highest compliment that my work ever received was bestowed by the Southern Pacific Railroad Company in the course of a controversy that Rockwell Kent had engaged them in. They wrote Mr. Kent, in extenuation of having published tracings of his Tierra del Fuego drawings to advertise a thing they called their Sunset Valley Route, that they did not know that Mr. Kent held a monopoly of that style of drawing, that they had seen the same style in the works of William Hogarth, Jr.

> *When I was a tiny lad,*
> *In a Noah's ark I had,*
> *Mr. Noah and his wife*
> *Led a calm, domestic life.*
> *Noah had legs—wooden pegs,*

NOAH'S ARKEOLOGY

by George S. Chappell

Not so, Mrs. N.
She was solid, to the ground,
And I fancied then
Women all were built that way,
   *   *   *   *
I was wrong, I'm glad to say!

NOAH'S ARKEOLOGY

Vanity Fair

SINCLAIR LEWIS

Born Sauk Center, Minnesota, February 7, 1885.
A.B., Yale, 1907. Worked as newspaper reporter, magazine
and book editor. Married. Author: *Main Street* (1920),
Babbitt (1922), *Arrowsmith* (1925), *Dodsworth* (1929).
Awarded Nobel Prize for literature, 1930. Home: Dorset,
Vermont.

BREAKING INTO PRINT appeared in Volume Two,
Part Two, new series of The Colophon; February, 1937.

Hotel Algonquin
59 to 65 West Forty-fourth Street
New York
January 12, 1937

Dear Mr. Adler:

*Before I start a book I make innumerable notes by hand.
The book itself I write on the typewriter with corrections afterwards by hand. And then have the thing copied by my secretary and
go over it again. It is frequently necessary for my secretary—Lou
Florey, who is taking this dictation—to copy a page five or six
times before it is finished.*

*As to dictation, I have never found it possible to dictate
anything except letters. I find that in dictation there is a serious*

tendency to repeat words and whole phrases. (As seen in first paragraph of this letter!)

I never read more than one proof—galley proof—and I am usually so sick of the book by that time that it is difficult even to read galley proof.

I am asking Mr. Florey to see if he can dig out a page of copy to send you for reproduction, but I won't guarantee your receiving it.

Yours sincerely,

Sinclair Lewis

of public official.

David

(Who has appeared at top of the stairs)

Please don't go, ~~Dad~~ Lorinda

Fowler

stomp
tend to it.

Lorinda

You do it. Please, ~~please wait till I have you~~ no! He's too an old pussy
need cat (hurt)
I'm certain there's something wrong about how Clarence. You've got
to find out. That man Swan will cover things up before you get
~~things~~ if you give him the chance (David appears head of stairs)

Fowler (David appears head of stairs)

All right
^I'll make sure he doesn't. Little's been a patient of mine since
I started. If there's anything wrong, I'll find it out. x
(He starts as he goes) — David
Your Dad's got to boss things.

~~they~~

Be careful, Fowler!

(FOWLER makes quick exit)

~~Lorinda~~

(To Mary)
Take David upstairs, Mary.

~~Mary~~

~~Comes son~~
(They exit) goes to

(LORINDA at phone)

Come on up-stairs,
Dad — got my
airplane working

Fowler

Got to go start
a little trouble
se now, old man. later

(Exit Fowler

Sinclair Lewis

ONE OF THE MOST CURIOUS questions about a writer, and one least often answered in biographies, is why he ever became a writer at all; why, instead of the active and friendly career of a doctor or a revolutionist or an engineer or an actor or an aviator (stage-driver it would have been in my early day), he should choose to sit alone, year after year, making up fables or commenting on what other and livelier citizens actually do. There is no problem about it when the writer's family circle is "artistic"—as with Hugh Walpole, collateral descendant of the great Horace and son of a brilliant bishop. He goes into his father's business somewhat as the grocer's son takes in his turn to the appalling existence of handing ketchup and cornstarch across a counter all day long. But how the devil did a Wells, a Bennett, a Howells, a Whitman ever, in their dreary middleclass boyhood homes, happen on writing as a desirable thing to do?

And how did a Harry Sinclair Lewis, son of an average doctor in a Midwestern prairie village, who never—but never!—heard at table any conversation except "Is Mrs. Harmon feeling any better?" and "Butter's gone up again" and "Mrs. Whipple told me that Mrs. Simonton told her that the Kellses have got a cousin from Minneapolis staying with them"—a youth who till he was ready to enter university had never seen any professional writer except the local country editors—how came it that at eleven he had already decided to become a short-story writer (an ambition, incidentally, that he never adequately carried out) and that at fourteen he sent off to *Harper's Magazine* what he believed to be a poem?

A good many psychologists have considered that in such a case, the patient has probably by literary exhibitionism been trying to get even with his schoolmates who could outfight, outswim, outlove, and in general outdo him. Of me that explanation must have been partly true, but only partly, because while I was a mediocre sportsman in Boytown, I was neither a cripple nor a Sensitive Soul. With this temptation to artistic revenge was probably combined the fact that my stepmother (since my father remarried when I was six, she was psychically my own mother) read to me more than was the village custom. And my father, though he never spoke of them, did have books in the house, and did respect them, as one who had been a school-teacher before he went to medical school.

Anyway, cause or not, there was, at eleven or earlier, the itch for scribbling. I must have been about ten when I regularly wrote a newspaper with the most strictly limited clientele in the world—myself. It had "departments," with not only a byline but a portrait of the department-editor. And at fifteen or so, I had a vacation-time job on the Sauk Center *Herald*, setting type, running a hand-press, and writing items (usually ending "A good time was voted by all") at the combined salary of nothing at all. Toward the end of summer when I asked for a rise, I was fired on the reasonable grounds that I wasn't worth what I had been getting. But I first had, that summer (perhaps in 1899 or 1900), the ecstasy of thus Breaking into Print.

By the time I had wriggled doubtfully into Yale, the itch was beyond prophylaxis. To writing, then, I devoted more eagerness than to any study, any sport, and on the *Yale Literary Magazine* and the *Yale Courant* I showered long mediaeval poems, with (O God!) ladys clad in white samite, mystic, won-der-ful; tales about Minnesota Swedes; and even two lyrics in what must have been terrible German. Perhaps half of them were accepted. The *Lit* was solemn, awesome, grammatical, traditional, and completely useless as a workshop; the *Courant* was frivolous, humble, and of the greatest use. . . . There was also a class in short-story writing in which the teacher, later author of a couple of fifth-rate novels, might have been pretty harmful if he had only been brighter.

During Yale I had my first acceptance by a real magazine—and it was critical, slightly scandalous, and, I can now see, inclined to make any number of worthy persons uncomfortable.

It was the time when Katherine Cecil Thurston's *The Masquerader* was the book of the hour, receiving as much quivering adulation as now lays itself before *Gone With the Wind*. At that time (end of my sophomore year, if I remember) I happened on an old novel, *The Premier and the Painter*, by Israel Zangwill but published under a pseudonym, and this tale was in general scheme and a good many separate scenes precisely like *The Masquerader*. I reported this in an article published in the now perished *The Critic*. . . . And that was the first of the many happy times that I have been damned, been put in my place, by the New York editorial writers.

My next adventure in what is termed "letters" was even more dubious. Having a natural distaste for children and an inability to communicate with them which has persisted to this day, I naturally took to writing "children's verse," of which a litter appeared in the women's magazines. As I remember these finger-exercises, compared with them A. A. Milne's pranks are Miltonic. And it was during college or just afterward that I sold my first short story—to a California magazine called *The Blue Mule*, and for the very satisfactory price of seven dollars. Commercially, at

A·B·C·D·E·F·G·H·I·J·K·M·S·L·N·O·P·Q·R·T·U·V·W·X·Y·Z

least, I had come on an impressive way since reportage on the Sauk Center *Herald*.

But all through college, with all this nonsense about Guinivere and Lancelot (a dumb hero if ever there was one), about the Little Ones and the gas-stove that was really a beastie, I was trying to try to plan a serious, a respectable novel. It was to be called *The Children's Children*, and it was an early guess at the four-generation novel that would, years later, with my having nothing at all to do with it, become only too ponderously plentiful. In my scheme, each generation was to revolt against the earlier, and move —from New Haven to Minnesota to California and then (in this I did a little anticipate a paradoxical migratory movement which then had only begun) rebound against the wall of the Pacific Ocean and back East again. I doubt if I ever wrote so much as ten pages of this opus, but out of planning it, seeing its distressing problems, I probably got more sense of writing than in all my spawn of scribbling for the magazines.

So out of college, out West as secretary to Grace Macgowan Cook—William Rose Benét and I shared a shack in Carmel when it was only a clearing among the pines—back East to work in a publishing house, and all the years from 1908 to 1914, trying to write my first actually completed novel, *Our Mr. Wrenn. Main Street*, which is always put down as my first book, happens to have been my seventh.

Wrenn, published in 1914, was a fair piece of light fiction; its soundest virtue that it did have an authentic sympathy with a very little Little Man; a New York clerkling, lonely and timid, who longed to "see the world," as we used to say in those days before the world became suicidal and dishevelled and generally not worth seeing. He inherited a fortune of a few hundred dollars; he started off world-seeing by cattle-boat to Liverpool and on foot through England; he became as retchingly homesick as I had been

[122]

on just the same sort of trip after freshman year in college; and he wisely returned to clerkship and littleness.

The book sold well enough—perhaps 3000 copies—and even had two or three cordial reviews. That, naturally, was enough to make the disease chronic and incurable.

So 1920, and *Main Street* and the damned photographs, interviews, invitations to lecture, nibbles (still resisted) from Hollywood, and all the rest of the clamor with which the world tries, inevitably, to keep a writer from his one job—which is writing. It has been a good job and, even when it has been rather sweaty and nerve-jangling, I have enjoyed it more than I would have enjoyed anything except pure research in a laboratory. Mind you, the writing itself has been as important to me as the product, and I have always been somewhat indifferent as to whether I have been working on a solemn novel or an impertinent paragraph for the *New Yorker*. I have never been a propagandist for anything, nor against anything save dullness. A good job—and not for gold would I recommend it as a career to any one who cared a hoot for the rewards, for the praise, for the prizes, for the embarrassment of being recognized in the restaurants, or for anything at all save the secret pleasure of sitting in a frowsy dressing-gown, before a typewriter, exulting in the small number of hours when the words (noble or ribald, it doesn't matter) come invigoratingly out in black on white, and the telephone doesn't ring, and lunch may go to the devil.

And as the recipe for writing, all writing, I remember no high-flown counsel but always and only Mary Heaton Vorse's jibe, delivered to a bunch of young and mostly incompetent hopefuls back in 1911: "The art of writing is the art of applying the seat of the pants to the seat of the chair." As for the others—let them go to Hollywood or to the "studios" of the N.B.C., and everything will be idealistic, and the literary caravan will march gaily on.

WILLIAM McFEE

Born London, England, June 15, 1881.

Educated in East Anglian School, Bury St. Edmunds, England. Worked as engineer both on land and sea. Served in the transport service during the World War, ending as a sublieutenant in the British Navy. Chief engineer, United Fruit Company, 1920-22. Married. Author *An Ocean Tramp* (1908), *Casuals of the Sea* (1916), *Harbors of Memory* (1921), *The Beachcomber* (1935). Home: Westport, Connecticut.

GETTING INTO PRINT appeared in Part One of The Colophon; February, 1930.

Westport, Conn.
December 19, 1936

Dear Elmer Adler:

It is never a bother to me to talk about myself. The first faint signs that people are no longer interested in me will throw me into a panic.

I therefore send you the following seriatim replies to your queries.

I write all my mss. by hand on yellow paper blocks because I derive some obscure sensuous satisfaction from the handling of a pen. I write my letters direct on an old typewriter, as thus.

[125]

A·B·C·D·E·F·G·H·I·J·K·L·**W**·**M**·N·O·P·Q·R·S·T·U·V·X·Y·Z

When the ms. is re-read, if it is a short article or review, my wife types it on a large formidable Underwood with appropriate carbons. If fiction, I send it to a lady expert in New York, who mails it direct to the office, returning the mss. and the carbon to me. When finishing The Beachcomber *in Miami I found it necessary to do the last 25,000 words in a week. I wrote, in longhand, 5 to 6,000 words each day, mailed it each morning air-mail to the lady in Brooklyn, who typed it at night as she received it, and we got in under the wire 24 hours ahead of the dead line. It gave me immense satisfaction because I had been thinking "You're old! You can't do it any more!"*

On one or two occasions I typed things for myself simply because I was so ashamed of them I hated to let anyone see them. I had been inveigled by my agent to do what he called "short shorts." I did five in about three days. He sold them all for immense sums, and one of them he has sold twice. But I was so shamed, etc. On another occasion I had a long short story that an editor was needing and my wife was ill after an operation, and I did it myself. I felt that nothing would ever make me like a typist's life.

I have never dictated. I have often wondered how it is done. I know a novelist in England who can neither spell nor punctuate, and she is successful. She dictates while sewing and her secretary attends to the punctuation, etc. To me it is incredible that anyone could get pleasure out of dictating. I can certainly see the effects of it in the style of those who dictate. I cannot even work with anyone else in the room!

I always try to get book proofs, but try and get them from an American publisher! I think the proof business is much better managed in England. The trouble over there is, they never seem to have any royalties.

[126]

Not many changes. With regard to the authors who like to make changes in page proofs, I refer you to the publishers for forcible remarks thereon. It is they who have brought in that cagey clause about the cost of corrections in proofs being borne by the author jointly with the house. This does not affect me much. My proof corrections consist of typographical errors, changes of colons (to which I am ridiculously partial because I like the look of them) to commas, deletion of commas that come out like a rash sometimes in my mss. and fights with proof readers who know more about Webster's Unabridged than about life. In general I destroy a much altered page of ms., and rewrite it. In general I wait, and wait, and wait until I know what I am doing. When an author tells us that he rewrites whole pages and corrects and recorrects, I feel like asking "Why the hell don't you wait and find out what you are doing?" This mad craze for doing so many words a day is the real reason, I fancy. Authors are almost childishly fond of seeing a stack of mss. There that's done! *In many cases it isn't done and it isn't sold even.*

Do you want the ms. of a novel or a story? I have nothing here. I can get lots of mss. from the man who did the Bibliography (James T. Babb, Esq.). He collects all my stuff, and nowadays I do not sell them but give them to him. He will loan you several interesting things. I can, however, dig up a ms. here perhaps. I inclose one.

I hope this covers everything you need for the book. With all good wishes for this time of year,

Sincerely

William McFee

William McFee

THERE can be no objection, at the beginning of a confession-story in which the ego must play the major role, if mention be made of the adventures of two authors of widely differing experience.

There are many writers, commercially successful, who protest acrimoniously that they know nothing about literature. They refuse to give the young people any assistance whatever. They are bad tempered on the subject of intellectuals and are contemptuous of the elaborate mechanism of publicity maintained by publishers to build up the reputation of their authors. Such a man is my good friend Joe Fitzhubert, to give him a name which is, I trust, an effective incognito.

Joe makes, with satisfying regularity, forty thousand dollars a year. He writes nothing but short stories. He writes only one kind of short story—the kind he can sell. He began by selling short stories after a career which included newspaper work, law-practice and semi-pro base-ball, whatever that may be. He is a boisterous writer, is Joe, popular with his public, and a great favorite with barbers, who read his stories while waiting for a customer. Joe doesn't care whether you think his stuff is good or not. His test of a short story is the number of hundreds of dollars he receives for it. So far as I can gauge he earns thirty-five cents a word, but he expects by the turn of the year to have raised this to fifty cents. He writes about twenty stories a year. He has three expensive cars, a house in Connecticut and a yacht at Fire Island where he spends the summer. He is entirely satisfied with his cars, his yacht and his career. He thinks a man who writes for a low-price magazine a fool. He admits the existence of what he calls "the carriage trade," but his ideal writer is one who caters to all classes of society from millionaires to morons. Nobody remembers Joe's stories once they have appeared. He does not remember them himself. He has made several collections of his stories in volume form, but something seems to be missing, once you take Joe's stories from their brilliant setting among all those advertisements of disinfectants, tooth-paste, motor cars, linoleum and sanitary goods. They seem, somehow, like last year's newspaper. Joe is good-humoredly contemptuous of publishers who make a noise over a sale of ten thousand copies of a book. His stories are probably devoured by ten million people.

Joe went into writing as what he calls "the easiest way." He read a lot of stories, decided that he could do better himself and promptly proved it. He discovered it was easy. He has never looked back. He makes forty thousand a year. In a little while, when his agent has closed that contract for talkie-scenarios made from Joe's mystery series, it will be seventy-five thousand. Joe's favorite song is a paraphrase of Eva Tanguay's famous ditty:

> *My style may be funny*
> *But it's getting me the money,*
> *So I don't care.*

Joe's method of writing is simplicity itself. He dictates to a secretary who operates a noiseless typewriter. If he wants to work when she is not there, he dictates into a dictaphone. When the secretary comes in the morning she takes it down from the machine while Joe is playing golf. He revises it in the afternoon. He says that Homer really wrote dime novels and Shakespeare would have used a dic-

A·B·C·D·E·F·G·H·I·J·K·L·**W**·M·N·O·P·Q·R·S·T·U·V·X·Y·Z

taphone if they had been on sale in those days. He thinks if
Milton had taken a course in short story writing he could
have made a fine series of *Paradise Lost* under the title of
The Sorrows of Satan. What Keats really needed, he insists,
was a good syndicate editor. And as for Conrad, Joe hasn't
patience to discuss him. Conrad couldn't write. Conrad,
according to Joe, spends all his time beating about the bush
instead of "cutting the cackle and coming to the 'orses,"
which means, I imagine, getting on with the story.

Enough of Joe. Let me turn now to another literary
acquaintance if I may be so bold. She is on what ought to
be the threshold of life. She is sixteen. Her parents are cul-
tured and literary. She was reared in the shadow of a great
university but she has never been to school. She was a child
wonder. She typed her first book, a fantastic allegorical
novel, at the age of nine. It has been published. A copy is
on my shelves. At thirteen she made a voyage in a schooner
and wrote a brilliant narrative which was published. I reviewed it. Through a friend I made Madeline's acquaintance. I also made the acquaintance of Madeline's mother.
Madeline's mother is one of those women who make extensive plans which include my own laborious, enthusiastic
and prolonged coöperation. The plan she had in mind at
this particular time was to take Madeline on a long cruise
to the Cannibal Islands, in a sailing ship. Madeline was to
write long brilliant letters to me and I was to get them published. They would get the royalties and I would get the
credit of sponsoring a child genius. When I pointed out
that Madeline was fourteen and would become a woman
very shortly the suggestion fell on deaf ears. I went so far as
to add that a child, instead of being spurred on to write,
should be held back for a few years. I might as well have
spoken to the wind in the chimney. Madeline's mother was
that kind of a woman. And the last I heard of Madeline
was that she had tried to throw herself out of the hotel window in some distant city. At sixteen Madeline is on the

[131]

threshold of disaster. In a year or two, by reason of an un-
wise premature development, she may never write another
line.

It would be hard to imagine two careers more widely
divergent, yet they have one quality in common with most
modern writers in America. As soon as Joe and Madeline
began to write at the ages, respectively, of twenty-nine and
nine, they achieved publication. The reason for narrating
their exploits lies in this quality. They are, for all their
differences in age, temperament and performance, part of
the alert, urgent, confident American scene. In this they
differ somewhat spectacularly from my own beginnings in
England.

It was one of the paradoxes of the Victorian Era, in
which I was born and grew up, that literature, which was
the national art, was regarded by the general public as
something outside of their own lives. There was no way by
which a young person afflicted with the desire to write,
could gain any useful information about the profession of
writing. The average young person's head, if mine be taken
as an example, contained a vague hodgepodge of notions.
Literature was conceived by us as an extraordinary mi-
crocosm. It was a town something like Oxford, with a slum
called Grub Street in which starving authors lived in
garrets. A river ran past the end of this street, into which
poets precipitated themselves in despair. At the other end
of the town briefless barristers wrote reviews of books written by well-known novelists like Anthony Hope, Marie
Corelli and Hall Caine, who lived in country mansions. At
an oriel window in one of the colleges of this dream city
Walter Pater sat writing imperishable prose. And at various
corners of respectable but poverty-stricken streets were red
post-boxes into which young geniuses were dropping their
manuscripts at dead of night.

The young person never felt that he belonged in this
place. Indeed if my own emotions are to be accepted as

typical of the literary beginner of those days, I felt as much of an outsider as does the tourist from Kansas when he is admitted to the buttery of Brasenose College or wanders through the ancestral chambers of Blenheim or Hatfield. To me there was an almost supernatural radiance surrounding anyone who even "wrote for the papers." How often have I pored over that fascinating character in the novels of those days, the young barrister who lived in chambers and who would come home to spend an evening reviewing half a dozen new novels! He generally finished up with a pipe and a glass of wine, and would spend an hour staring into the fire thinking of the Honourable Betty Blundell-Blandish, whom he had met at Ascot. He was a remarkable chap, that briefless barrister, and he is largely responsible for my own cowardly procrastination and reluctance at that time to make more than one or two timid advances in the business of writing. It did not seem to me that the resources within myself were sufficient to compete with him.

This is all the more noteworthy because at school I was always writing. One of my stories may be found in the school magazine for 1897, and a terrible thing it was. It gave me no confidence to see my own words in print. I can remember the Fifth Form master coming round to my desk during preparation and looking over my shoulder as I corrected the long galley-proofs of that story. He had no great opinion of me and so great was the pressure of public opinion in an English school that I was inclined to agree with him. He was amused. He made a jocose comment upon my new dignity and added a caustic remark to the effect that if I were to put as much beef into my work as I did into that stuff, I might amount to something in the world.

This illuminating phrase expresses exactly the general attitude of every one with whom I associated at school and at home. Within a few months of leaving school I was writing, for a local paper, a weekly half column, supposedly humorous. Inspiration failing the half column failed, and not long after the paper itself failed, which may have had its cumulative effect on the author of these disasters. My mother, for one, was resigned when she heard that my contributions were no longer wanted. To her it was a sorry waste of time and likely to lead me to a pauper's grave. She wanted me to amount to something, to quote the Fifth Form master, and it was entirely beyond her intelligence to understand how that could be achieved by writing. The neighbors, had they known or cared, would have agreed with her.

The paradox referred to on an earlier page was this— that all these people believed in education. To have "a splendid education" was a most desirable thing. And they all read books. We even had "evenings" with various authors at the local literary society at which a classic like Thackeray or a modern novelist like Hall Caine or Marie Corelli, would be discussed. But they were authors, we were the public. We never saw them and the mechanics of publicity was only dimly understood in those days. They were far-off, living in a social and artistic heaven, and the notion never occurred to anyone that a humble and somewhat tongue-tied bumpkin like myself could enter into those magic realms. This feeling has never worn off. Even now I have a faint suspicion that, compared with the great mandarins of those days, and their umbrella-holders, the briefless barristers who reviewed their books, I am no more than an impostor. They achieved a dignity, an inaccessible grandeur, which will remain forever beyond the writer of these lines. That the books they wrote were rubbish and that their names are already passing from memory in no way diminishes their formidable prestige in my consciousness. And so I have ever retained the conviction that I broke into print very much as a burglar breaks into a mansion or—to improve the metaphor—as a tramp breaks into a chicken house; and that my immunity will continue only so long as

passé jokes, and offering us a new goods the same old reach-me-downs of the nineties, Tolstoi was always quoting "The Bond." Shaw quotes Shaw, to the discomfiture of the present Shaws. And the sight of a the person making fun of himself, for our amusement makes one us turn away in shocked embarrassment.

The best thing to do, to take the taste of these plays out of one's mouth, is to read Bernard Shaw. "Man and Superman," for example, "Candida," "Cæsar..."

the real owners of the place remain unaware of my depre-
dations. I am, in fact, unable to feel as I imagine a genuine
author ought to feel. I suspect even editors and publishers
of the physiological feat of uttering honeyed words with
their tongues in their cheeks. No measure of achievement
appears to diminish the sense of being an unlicensed hawker
of literary wares. Or to revert to my previous metaphor,
having broken into print I am everlastingly apprehensive
of being thrown out.

It is obvious that a man of so little confidence will not
have the courage to conceal his lowly literary origins. He
will certainly be unable to deny having arrived on deck—
to change the metaphor once again—through the cabin
window and not through the hawse-pipe. In other words,
I read enormously and then lived vigorously. My friend
Joe Fitzhubert will assure you in high good humor that a
couple of years at a newspaper copy-desk are better for a
writer's muscles than the same time spent in the libraries of
universities. He probably has a sound case. I am not here to
argue, but to confess. The flaw in Joe's logic is that to me
writing is a pleasure, whereas to him it is a job to be done
and gotten out of the way. To me writing grows out of and
is an integral part of my existence. I have no real existence
apart from the turmoil which produces, at irregular inter-
vals, books. To Joe it is a profitable business, which he in-
tends to abandon as soon as the stock-market and some
parcels of real-estate enable him to do so.

I am not here to criticize Joe because I suspect he may
be right. The point is that I couldn't follow Joe's example
if I tried for fifty years. I would only do clumsily what Joe
does with sinewy ease and a slick finish. Joe thinks differ-
ently. He writes me big-brotherly letters urging me to write
for the magazines that pay big money. He is convinced that
if I could only abandon the highbrow point of view I would
find it as easy as he does. It is his whimsical fancy to maintain that "if the real writers ever discover how easy it is,"

poor fakers like himself will be in the poorhouse in no time. That is his democratic way.

Good temper may alleviate but it can never destroy these literary cleavages. We who were born and bred in the literary tradition of England are artists, or amateurs, depending on your point of view, because we would write whether we made any money at it or not. So it follows that so many Englishmen are trained in trades and professions far divorced from writing and remain faithful to them long after they are achieving success in letters. In America one is startled, in spite of the frequency with which it happens, to meet young men who have selected novel writing as their profession and are settling seriously to work on leaving college. To have mocked the fates thus insolently would have been inconceivable to me. Many of my early manuscripts have never been sent to any publisher or editor. And I went to sea, not with the conscious design of accumulating material for stories, but in obedience to an obscure but powerful passion to see the world. Love, money and the desire to wander were mixed in equal proportions. But there was no conscious aim. All three motives were separate and distinct from the desire to write. I thought well of myself, but I have forgotten, if I ever knew, the reason why. I was soft with office work and I was not in sympathy with the men who are to be found on ships. Looking back I see nothing admirable in the youth that was myself save the passion for fine literature. At that time I was not even romantically interested in the sea, in the sense that so many Americans seem to be. It was my family profession. And when I try to recall just what set me off writing my first published book I am at a loss. Let me try again. . . .

My first dinner ashore in Italy. It was Leghorn. I sat and watched an Italian officer eat macaroni and pull the *fiasco* of "Asti" towards him as it swung in its bracket with gimbals like the lamp in my cabin. I had learned a little

Italian. He said, looking at me, "*Sera, Signore.*" And then, still looking at me, he added "No? You are English, yes?" I knew enough Italian to tell him I did not speak Italian. He called the *padrone* and they laughed together.

The boat taking me back to the ship in the moonlight. The round bullet-head of the second engineer, smoking a clay pipe, looking down at me as I came up the rope ladder. He had just been married before we left England. He asked me if I had seen any signorinas.

The moonlight again on the harbor of Aghilhas in Southern Spain. A coaster moving out like a ship of silver on a sea of dreams. The second engineer seated on the hatch asking me if I had seen any senoritas.

The port of Caen, where we were loading iron ore. One of the winches broken. Working nearly all night on it. As we finished the second engineer saying there would be no chance of seeing any mademoiselles.

Character, it seems, was what I was after, even if it were only my own that finally emerged in those first pages. And when the book was finished, I cannot remember anything of its early vicissitudes. It was accepted by the first publisher who read it. While it was being submitted I had gone up for my examination and had passed easily. I was still in love, but nothing seemed likely to come of it because I had no position and no money. And when another ship was offered I sailed. I remember a telegram coming to the sea port where the ship was loading coal for Las Palmas. It was from the agent, who wanted to know if I would accept twenty-five pounds for the book rights. I would have accepted five pounds. Twenty-five pounds was three months' wages.

We were away a year. We discharged coal in Las Palmas, went across to Philadelphia and loaded case oil for Kobe, went down from Japan to Java and loaded sugar for Boston. From there we went to Savannah and loaded cotton for Liverpool. A fine voyage, if you were single. We were in Boston at Christmas 1908. I can remember walking through the snowy streets and looking in a bookseller's window. My book, *Letters From an Ocean Tramp*, was on sale. I did not buy a copy. I had spent twenty-five pounds in Japan and needed money when I reached home. But I was pleased to see it. In fact, it gave me more pleasure than any other experience of that time. I had good reviews, but the book did not sell. Later the publishers sold a large remainder to a bookseller, the Times Book Club, I believe. Now the book is rare. But at the time the publishers were disappointed and refused to have anything more to do with me. I was writing *Casuals of The Sea* but they would have nothing more to do with me. I passed another examination and went to sea again. My love affair petered out. I went on writing *Casuals of The Sea*. Seven years were to pass before I broke into print again. Looking back, I fancy they were the happiest years in my life. I had broken into print, and I went on living.

HENRY LOUIS MENCKEN

Born Baltimore, Maryland, September 12, 1880.
Educated privately and at the Baltimore Polytechnic,
1896. Worked on various newspapers, later editing successively, with George Jean Nathan, *The Smart Set* and *The
American Mercury*. Widower. Author *A Book of Prefaces*
(1917), *The American Language* (1918; 4th edition, corrected, enlarged, and rewritten, 1936), *Prejudices* (six
series, 1919-27), *Treatise on the Gods* (1930). Home: 1524
Hollins Street, Baltimore, Maryland.

ON BREAKING INTO TYPE appeared in Part
One of The Colophon; February, 1930.

1524 Hollins St.
Baltimore.
December 21, 1936.

Dear Adler:

Here are my answers to your questions:

*1. I work directly on the typewriter, and never use a
pen—in fact, writing by hand has got so painful to me that it has
become next door to impossible.*

2. My copy is ordinarily re-typed by my secretary.

3. I never dictate anything save letters.

4. The copy that I send to the printer is almost letter-

[139]

perfect, and so my author's corrections are inconsiderable. In my magazine days I never asked for galley proofs at all. I worked directly on the page proofs.

5. I seldom, if ever, make any considerable changes in my text after it has been set up.

6. I am enclosing a typical piece of manuscript. It is the typescript of an article written for the Baltimore Evening Sun *a couple of weeks ago. As you will notice, it is clean enough to go to the printer as it stands. Nevertheless, I usually have such scripts retyped.*

I am entertaining at the moment an attack of bronchitis. It doesn't seem to be serious, but it is certainly most uncomfortable. God help us all in 1937!

Yours,

H. L. Mencken

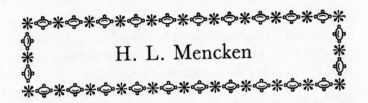

H. L. Mencken

ACCORDING TO Vincent Starrett, who should know, my *Ventures Into Verse*, Baltimore, 1903, is one of the rarest of modern American books. Every now and then I hear of a sale at a fantastic price: the last one, as I recall it, was beyond $150. Such news naturally caresses an author's gills; nevertheless, I find myself somewhat disquieted, for the book, in the main, is dreadful stuff, and any buyer who happens to be a man of taste must needs conclude that he has been rooked, and lay some of the blame for the swindle upon me. In my defense I can only say that I was young when the thing was published and even younger when most of it was written, and that the wisdom which now radiates from me was late in developing. In 1903 I was not a metaphysician, but a newspaper reporter, and in 1895 I was a schoolboy.

Some of the verse in the book goes back to the latter year, and one or two pieces were probably written, at least in first draft, in 1894. I was then torn between two aspirations: one to be a chemist and the other to be a poet. Neither seemed possible of realization, for my father had his heart set upon taking me into his tobacco business, and there was no apparent way of escape. But I kept on playing in my laboratory and writing verse, putting one hope against the other. In 1894, when I was 14, I invented a platinum toning solution for photographs, and at once put it into a solemn article. Whether or not I submitted it to the photographic magazines I can't remember: at all events it was not printed. At the same time I began a furious verse-writing, and for a while, like many another ambitious young poet, tried to produce at least one poem a day.

They fell into two classes. Half were experiments in the old French forms that were then so popular, and the rest were imitations of Kipling, then the god of all literate youngsters. I made no effort to sell this stuff, but put it in a drawer, and there most of it still remains. In 1896 the tobacco business gobbled me, and thereafter, for three years, I wrote next to nothing. Chemistry, too, faded into the background: I was in training as a business man, and my father was a diligent and exigent teacher. At the beginning of 1899, when I was eighteen, he died suddenly, and a week later I applied for a job on the old Baltimore *Herald*, now no more. I was put on trial immediately, and in a few months had a regular assignment. I remained with the *Herald* until it suspended publication, in 1906, becoming in succession Sunday editor, city editor, managing editor and editor-in-chief.

During my early days as a reporter, in 1900, my manner of writing news attracted the attention of the late Col. A. B. Cunningham, then chief editor of the *Herald*, and he proposed that I take over a weekly column on the editorial page, and therein disport myself in prose and verse. In that remote day columnists were still rare, and their present imperial honoraria were unheard of. My stipend was $14 a week, and my heavy duties as a somewhat starrish reporter kept on. Naturally enough, it was sometimes hard for me to fill my column, especially after it began to run twice a week instead of once. So I had recourse to my drawer full of schoolboy verse, and a great deal of it got into the *Herald* in 1900 and 1901. It was mainly banal, but so was nearly all the other newspaper verse of that time. Col. Cunningham liked it, and early in 1900 raised my wages to $18.

There was in those days an artist on the *Herald* named

number of absurdities. Thus, if a man buys 100 shares of stock
today and sells it tomorrow at a loss of $1000 he can deduct the whole
$1000 from his income, whereas if he bought the stock for investment
in 1925 and hugged it through boom and depression he may deduct only 30% of his
                                                                 patriotically
loss. To be sure, there is a compensatory provision he must pay
a tax on profits that runs the same
way, and moreover, he is unable to claim a loss of more than $2000 above his
profits, but nevertheless the whole section is irrational and ought to be
amended. (including the present subscriber)
If, as many people believe, stock market speculation is
essentially anti-social and ought to be put down, then an
easy way would be to soak all speculative profits on a heavy scale, beginning,
                                                              90% on
say, with 50% for those made within two or three months, and running to 100% on
those made within a month. Certainly it would be to the public interest
to separate speculative profits very sharply from investment profits and to the former
especially among the

The New Deal theory that too much saving,
rich, is one of the causes of depressions has not been reflected, so far, in
the Revenue Act. It allows no exemptions for personal expense, and even

John Siegel, a youngster of my own age. Not infrequently he illustrated my column, and so we became good friends. In 1902, when I was made Sunday editor, we were thrown together constantly. Another artist on the staff was Charles S. Gordon, and he too became one of my intimates. A third young man who hung about the place was Jim Beek, who knew something about advertising and engraving, and he in turn had a friend named Marshall, a printer. The five of us—Siegel, Gordon, Beek, Marshall and I—met often, both at the *Herald* office and in the adjacent saloons. We were all young and full of schemes. Siegel was preparing to go to Paris to study painting. Gordon chafed at his routine duties on the *Herald*. Beek and Marshall dreamed of owning a printing plant. And I was beginning to harbor literary ambitions, for some of my verse, too pretentious for the *Herald*, had been getting into the magazines, and with it a number of short stories.

One night, while we were drinking beer in a saloon, Marshall said he thought the time was ripe for setting up his printing office. The town printers, he said, were all old-fashioned; they seemed to know nothing about the new typography that was making a stir elsewhere. He had with him some specimens of that new typography, and they made a vast impression on all of us. In half an hour Marshall, Beek and Gordon had formed a partnership, with Marshall told off to do the printing, Beek to fetch the customers, and Gordon to do the art work. Siegel was left out because he was going to Paris, and I because I was neither a printer, a man of business nor an artist.

Within a week a small office was rented, presses and type were put in, and Beek was on the street soliciting trade. At once he found that potential customers wanted to be shown. It was all well enough to tell them that the new style of printing was swell, and to show them specimens of it from New York, England and Germany; what they demanded to see was what the firm of Marshall, Beek and

Gordon could do. So it became necessary to print something for their delectation, and that involved finding suitable copy. The three came to me for counsel, and I at once suggested that they do a book of my short stories: I had printed enough in the magazines to make a lovely volume. But there were obvious objections to that. The first was that short stories were straight copy, and would give Marshall little chance to display his talent for beautiful composition. The second was that such a book as I proposed would run to 250 pages, and would cost more than the new firm had to invest. Moreover, it would take more type than lay in the cases. The thing, obviously, had to be hand-set. It would not do to abandon that lovely Caslon for the poor faces which the linotype then offered.

Someone, as a way out, suggested that a book of verse be substituted for the short stories—a book of no more than 50 pages, elegantly hand-set by Marshall and decorated by Siegel and Gordon. It seemed a good idea, but I was inclined to balk. Most of my verse, I protested, was poor newspaper stuff; I had written only a few better things for the magazines. But there were plenty of arguments against that. No one read verse, anyhow—and certainly not business men. The thing would not go any further than Baltimore—and Baltimore had already digested and survived my worst. Marshall allowed that he fairly itched to fall upon the composition. The irregular lines would give him a grand chance, and he would produce a masterpiece. Siegel and Gordon promised to do their damnedest. Next morning the project was under way, and within a week the book was set up. I spent two hours confecting the title-page and two more pasting clippings on copy-paper. It was a quick job, and the critical faculty was in abeyance. At twenty-two I was to see my first book! It came out toward the end of April, 1903. I was not twenty-three until the following September.

Unfortunately, it cost more than Marshall had estimated, and when the time came to buy paper the infant firm found itself somewhat embarrassed. Thirty dollars, it appeared, stood between the book and disaster. I supplied the thirty dollars, and took half of the edition as my share. How many copies that ran to I can't recall, but it was certainly not much beyond a hundred. Most of them were bound in brown paper, with labels printed red on white, but a few—probably forty altogether—were bound by Marshall in binder's boards, with red backs and the same labels. Beek distributed the firm's copies among potential customers, and took some orders on the strength of them. Mine I divided into two halves, presenting the first half to friends and sending out the other to reviewers. Perhaps it deserves to be remembered by the historians of critical science in America that every paper which noticed the book at all praised it as good! One of them, I remember, was the New York *Sun*, then the most intelligent newspaper in the land!

How many copies survive I don't know—probably not many. The same one tends to bob up over and over again, bringing a larger price each time. Eight or ten years ago occasional copies were to be encountered in Baltimore, dredged out of lumber-rooms, but then the alert Baltimore dealer, Meredith Janvier, issuing from his lair in picturesque Hamilton Street, made a thorough search of the town, and when he had finished the supply was exhausted. It was about that time that the copies in the public libraries —perhaps five or six in all—were neatly stolen. One day, just as the news began to go about that the book could be sold, I met an old acquaintance on the street in Baltimore and he told me that he had a copy. He asked me if I would be offended if he turned it into cash. I told him no, and urged him to go to Janvier immediately, for the buying price was then $20, and I believed it would shrink to fifty cents, once the cackle over my dreadful verse had died down. Lately this punctilious Baltimorean got news of a sale at $140, and he has been giving me black looks ever since. Obviously, he shares the common belief that an author gains something when his dead books bring high prices. Ah, that it were so! I'd be richer than I am, and maybe chaster. As it is, all I get is the uneasy feeling that many a collector, bled by the current price, consoles himself by roaring over my youthful follies.

Let him console himself also with the assurance that there will never be a second edition. The copyright expires on April 30, 1931. Promptly at high noon of April 30, 1930, I shall make application in due form of law for a renewal for twenty-eight years. And if, before that time, my colloids turn to gas, then my executors will make the application for me.

CHRISTOPHER MORLEY

Born Haverford, Pennsylvania, May 5, 1890.
A.B., Haverford College, 1910. Rhodes Scholar, New College, Oxford, 1910–13. Worked on editorial staffs of publishing houses, magazines, and newspapers. Contributing editor, *Saturday Review of Literature*. Married. Author *Parnassus on Wheels* (1917), *The Haunted Book Shop* (1919), *Where the Blue Begins* (1922). Home: Roslyn Heights, L. I.

THE EIGHTH SIN appeared in Part Three of The Colophon; September, 1930.

It took a little extra effort to get this composite answer:

> *The Saturday Review of Literature*
> *25 West 45th Street, New York*
> *January 28, 1937*

My dear old Elmer,

> *Fantastic soul that you are—did my humble silence not convey to you that it was in itself an answer to your question?*

> *Bless your heart; the most valuable writing habit I have is not to answer questions about my writing habits. People who keep on answering questions (and I assure you that there are a great many such questions because the American public will always have an idea that there is some secret trick) very soon don't have time to do any writing.*

A·B·D·E·F·G·H·I·J·K·L·N·C·M·O·P·Q·R·S·T·U·V·W·X·Y·Z

I myself don't have much time for writing but I intend to keep on trying.

Good luck, and don't think this rude or evasive; it is only plain simple truth such as one utters to a friend.

Yours for Colophon

Christopher

February 1, 1937

Dear old Elmer,

The funny thing is that I thought I was *playing ball! It seemed to me that my letter would be an amusing (and unusually honest) contribution to the symposium. Even if all the other nineteen participants show themselves as egotists, why should I?*

No workman is likely to talk very intelligently about the technical details of his work; they depend upon instinct and practice which have trained themselves to become subconscious.

You know perfectly well, and so should the others, that the important part of writing goes on entirely in the mind before the hand touches paper.

*The only technical minutia in my own practice which can conceivably interest any one is this: I use a fountain pen but never as a fountain pen. I use it as a dipping pen, because dipping the pen in the ink gives you time enough to think and not so much time that you know you are thinking.—*Never use typewriter to compose; only to rewrite.

The gross details of manuscript preparation and proof correction belong in any beginner's manual and frankly I think it outrageous to call upon experienced people to discuss such piddling picayunes!

Now Elmer, you are an old rogue. I am just in the final phrensy of finishing a two-years' job in helping to edit the

[148]

A·B·D·E·F·G·H·I·J·K·L·N·C·M·O·P·Q·R·S·T·U·V·W·X·Y·Z

new Bartlett *and you must attribute to that anything that looks like nervous tension. But you know that I am right in this matter and I am sure these two letters will be the most sensible contribution you will get.*

Yours always,

Christopher

Christopher Morley

S WEET *are the uses of procrastination*. By delaying this promised memorandum several months it has happened that I have twice lately visited bookshops of the sort that I most esteem. On a day of golden heat I found myself at Mendoza's on Ann Street, and down in the cool cellar where few customers penetrate. That is the true sort of *rathskeller*, which must mean a cellar for wisdom, for council, for deliberation. I don't know why Ike Mendoza is always rather bashful about his basement and has to be coaxed to let me go down there. It is a noble place, and long ago the icepick he keeps there suggested to me a plot for a murder story—never written—of the two collectors who came to blows down there over a first edition. One stabbed the other in the colophon.

I cry *pfui* upon bookbuyers who only know the Uptown edition shoppes, all laid out for the tony trade, and are not aware of romance with golden loot (as Keats nearly said) in such byways as Ann Street.

And today, a wet weather, a damp drizzling sweetness, was such a day as Charing Cross Road knows in spring; a day of tender mists, a day that softened cheeks and foreheads to exquisite bloom; I wonder if the editors of this gazette, hard grizzled men stooped over collations and micrometers, know how beautiful a day it was? A London day, and only collectors really know what that means. In that cool dampness of air, eyes and complexions show a clarity, a childish lustre, the dear appeal of grace. On such a day, a day that seemed fresh from the pages of Dick Le Gallienne, I found my way again—for the first time in fourteen years—to Max Maisel's bookstore on Grand Street. It was there, fourteen years ago, I first discovered Walt Whitman's *Complete Prose*: the least-known American classic, I have always called it, and with justice, for at this moment it is o.p.—I wanted to get another copy, and Max didn't have it: but we had a good time; and he *did* have Tolstoy's *A Confession, and What I Believe*, to replace my copy which got away from me lang syne.

I haven't done enough trapesing in bookshops in recent years. Like the Lady of Shalott, the curse is come upon me. For having been innocently enthusiastic about books in my youth, I have been inundated with them. Parcels from the Book of the Month Club descend upon me almost daily; at a cautious computation some four hundred volumes a year from that source alone are delivered to the foundering members of its committee.

But all this is irrelevant. I began to say that just by chance, at Mendoza's I came upon a grimy little copy of *The Eighth Sin*. And by chance also I learned afterward the history of that particular copy; how it had been worth forty quid in London to someone very dear to me; and how he, bless him, had been a little anxious for fear I should think him mercenary for having sold it. It would be quite impossible to tell you the tender feeling one has for so completely innocent a little pamphlet, and the feeling of amazed gratification to know it could exert itself so substantially in an hour of need.

Just opposite the stone busts that palisade the Sheldonian (whether they are Roman emperors, Greek philomaths, or Christian apostles, no one knows; they are best remembered among the younger sort as having globuled with perspiration when Zuleika Dobson came to Oxford) is a famous bookshop, Blackwell's. One of the first phe-

nomena noticed by young Oxonians was the fact that Mr.
Blackwell made a habit of occasionally publishing collections of undergraduate verse. These little booklets were
bound in paper, sold (if at all) for a shilling each, and the
author made a contribution toward the printing bill. I remember offhand *Ignes Fatui* and *Metri Gratia* by Philip
Guedalla of Balliol and *Play Hours with Pegasus* by A. P.
Herbert of New College, which appeared in Blackwell's
window in 1911 or thereabouts. I myself in the spring of
1912 was writing a lot of verse, and collecting many politely
worded slips beginning *The Editor regrets* . . . It is a commonplace of later criticism to observe that there was a genuine renaissance of English poetry in the year 1912. But
I did not have to wait ten years to know that: I knew it
then. I was sure of it: I was helping to write it, and on the
red-baize-covered table beside the lofty window (overlook-
ing the old wall and New College bell-tower and the white
cherry tree) I looked at these editorial denials severely disappointed at such unity of sentiment in diversity of print.
I could never quite make up my mind which was the most
perfect Rejection Slip. Of the English, I give the palm to
The English Review—"The Editor regrets that he is reluc-
tantly compelled to return the enclosed MS." But nothing
can ever surpass the gentlemanly finesse of the *Atlantic
Monthly*. "If, as in the present instance, it proves impracti-
cable to accept such a manuscript because of the necessity
of giving precedence to other contributions, the editors beg
to be excused from the ungracious task of criticism." I have
a choice little anthology of Rejection Slips from those days.
I think the earliest one I saved was from *Lippincott's Magazine*—which some of you have already forgotten. It is dated
July 13, 1909, and records the return of "Three Poems."
And the Editor has written, evidently in answer to the
young versifier's inquiry, "If MSS are legibly written it is
the only requisite." Alas, not the only requisite. I know

very well how legibly my "Ode on the History of Lake Champlain" was written; but it was never printed.

But on the 8th of May 1912 the lyric renaissance began to look up. It is all very well for Mr. Canby and Mr. Van Doren to remark that the first twangle of the lyre was the founding of *Poetry* in Chicago, or Vachel Lindsay's *Rhymes for Bread*, or John Masefield's *Everlasting Mercy*, or Mitchell Kennerley's publication of *The Lyric Year* containing Miss Millay's *Renascence* (and many other fine things). I know better. So far as I was concerned the Renaissance began one spring morning when (as usual) I went down three flights of stone stairs, in dressing gown and pyjamas, to see if there was any mail on the slab at the bottom. There was a letter from *T. P.'s Magazine*. Here it is (you don't think I would have lost that letter)—

> *8th May, 1912.*
> *The Editor of T. P.'s Magazine would be pleased to use Mr. Morley's poem entitled "Rondeau" if he would accept 7/6d for same.*

That was the first time I was ever paid money for writing anything. It was the custom of meditative youth, in those spring days, to walk around the college garden in dressing gown and slippers before returning to one's room for bath (in a tin tub) and breakfast. Those who have seen an Oxford garden before breakfast, on a May morning, when you have just had your first poem accepted, will remember what life feels like. And in the immediate background you must imagine a spring vacation which had been spent in three of the most glamorous regions on earth—a garret in the Latin Quarter, the forest of Fontainebleau, and the daisy fields of Devonshire. The output of rondeaux had been lively. On the outskirts of Moret-sur-Loing there is a forest edge where two other young students and I used to spread rugs and lie under a walnut tree looking over the April valley snowed with fruit blossoms. One of these lads was a mathematician and growing a beard, one a Scandi-navian gymnosophist who used to strip and run miles of physical culture through the *allées* of the forest wearing only heavy cowhide boots. He was living on lemon juice and toast and praying to the norns. And I, supposedly studying history, was mostly thinking about R. L. Steven-son and putting the rondels of Charles d'Orleans into verse translation. Marvellous, marvellous days, of first life, first love, first wine and first literature.

Such were some of the backgrounds of the innocent *8th Sin*. The letter from *T. P.'s Magazine* persuaded me to be not less bold than my friends Messrs. Guedalla and Herbert. In October 1912 I sent my little sheaf of rhymes to Mr. Blackwell. He wrote and asked me to come in and talk it over.

Good Mr. Blackwell, the founder of that admirable business, died some years ago and the traffic is now con-ducted by his charming son Basil, who has not forgotten (nor will he) the folk-dance picnics up the Cherwell River on summer evenings. Surely it might have been unneces-sary to write poetry in Oxford; we lived it. To fill several punts and canoes with boys and girls and supper-hampers, to go idling upstream a few miles, brew tea with alcohol stoves, then the cold salmon and cucumbers from Buol's, and to dance *The Butterfly* or *Jenny Pluck Pears* in a sunset meadow: this was certainly to have all the fun of the Tu-dors. Basil was the unselfish one; he was adept on a sort of tin whistle so he patiently furnished the music while the rest of us capered. The skylarks of those Cherwell meadows had to keep twittering aloft in upper sunshine, for we were thumping their homeland with the pattern of *Rufty Tufty* and *Mage on a Cree*. Many a lark must have been wing-weary when he could finally come down to his tussocked nest on earth.

What I remember best of my bashful interview with Mr. Blackwell senior besides his pink face and white hair

and extreme politeness was his asking me to put in some
more commas. I like your poems, he said, but there don't
seem to be any commas in them. Perhaps you don't use
commas much in America?

It was easy to oblige him in this; I haven't any copy to
refer to, but I believe the frequency of commas is about
normal. I don't remember how many he printed; either
250 or 350 I imagine. They were ready at the end of November, and the small gray booklet had its day in that
well-known window opposite the Roman emperors, who
did not perspire. Among the steerage passengers in the
Mauretania that December were a number of copies. When
I say steerage I mean it literally: there were three of us who
crossed in her in the third class, to spend Christmas at
home. So, with proper humility, did the *8th Sin* first come
to New York. And I should remark, since the peccadillo
has happened to amuse collectors, that to make the item
complete there should go with it a small card that the author had printed to accompany it, chastely saying "*With
the Apologies of the Perpetrator.*" I have just one of those cards
left, pasted in a scrapbook, and I suppose I ought to give
it to Burton Emmett, the only begetter of these confessions.

The only other importation of the booklet, in bulk,
was eight or nine years later. I was working on the *New
York Evening Post* when I got a letter from Basil Blackwell
saying that ten (I think it was ten, it may have been twelve)
copies of the *8th Sin* had turned up in his cellar. (Blackwell's, like Mendoza's, and all other real bookshops, had a
cellar.) He didn't believe they were salable but he was having a housecleaning and would I care for them? In short he
sent them to me with his affectionate compliments; and
astounded me by adding that now that the episode of the
8th Sin was finally worked off there was a small royalty
owing to me—I speak by memory only; I think it was
about five shillings and sixpence.

The package duly arrived; I called for it at the old

City Hall P.O., paid a duty on it which was practically the same as the amount of the royalty. As usual I was hard up, and Eddie Newton had burst into print not long before with the *Amenities* in which he had uttered a rousing view-hallo about the *8th Sin*. Here was I with ten copies on my hands. I went to call on James F. Drake, the Governor as I like to call him, and explained the situation. I offered him all ten copies at $5 each.

The Governor is a shrewd man. Ten copies of the *8th Sin* looked to him like about nine more copies than world, flesh or devil would have any use for. And as a matter of fact he already had one copy which had come to him from the library of the late Frank Dempster Sherman (to whom I had given it; do you remember Frank Sherman's very lovely lyrics? the Austin Dobson of Columbia University). In short, the Governor didn't relish my proposal. He suggested something, to which my thought was, if they were only worth that I might as well give 'em away. Which I did. I gave three or four to colleagues in the *Evening Post* office and presented the rest to Frank Shay, the imaginative bookseller of Christopher Street, because I knew it would amuse him to have them on his shelves. Speaking of Collectors' Items, I wish I knew what became of the famous door in Frank's bookshop which all his customers autographed.

The *8th Sin* was, as Cowley said of his juvenilia, "commendable extravagance in a boy." My severe tutor Mr. Herbert Fisher of New College remarked when I gave him a copy that "to write poetry in youth improves one's prose style in old age and I remember hearing Walter Pater commend the practice on that ground." The improvement of my prose, or old age even, were certainly far from my happy mind in that halcyon period. One episode alone, of many oddities associated with the booklet, would have justified its existence. I received a letter once from a gentleman in Cleveland, then unknown to me, saying he had come across the pamphlet somewhere and would I sign it for him. I wrote that it was a little curio of very specially personal flavor to me, and I had never signed a copy except for old friends to whom I had given it. Some years later, the incident having evaporated from my mind, I was in Cleveland, and was startled by the extreme courtesy and hospitable mien of a kindly and delightful but unidentified kinsprit who met me at the train, took me to a club, led me to a small bar-room, and produced a small leather case that looked like a prayer-book. Inside this case were four tall glass tubes, with silver-cork stoppers; and inside the tubes some of the best Bourbon one ever enjoyed. I enormously admired the outfit, and unguardedly expressing my admiration he insisted on my accepting it. I was abashed at so noble a gift, and babbled something about perhaps some day being able to get even with him. From another pocket he then drew a copy of the *8th Sin* and my letter of declination.

Needless to say we called for pen and ink on the spot; and by the time the test-tubes were empty we would either of us have signed anything anyone laid before us. I am sure that Jack Crawford, judge of bourbon and bibliophily, will not mind my recalling this beginning of our friendship—

It is customary for authors to remark, with a pretended sadness, that they themselves get no advantage from the hazard of new fortunes that sometimes attaches to their prentice opuscules. But anyone with the soul of a collector, who knows how precious and fantastic a web of associations a book can spin about itself, realizes what deep and humorous pleasure there is in causing actual sums of money to change hands among grown-up and cautious people. Circulation is good for money, as it is for books and people. I am sorry for books, as I am for people, who suffer no vi-

cissitudes. We have known the condition described by
Dick Le Gallienne when the poet—

> *filled with shame and grief*
> *Sold his last Swinburne for a plate of beef,*

and we have known hallucinations of apparent solvency.
But neither in the dignity of the Anderson Galleries nor in
the silence of Basil Blackwell's cellar have the *8th Sin* and I
misunderstood one another. The title itself, if you know its
allusion, is cheerfully humble. And the perpetrator, if he
thinks of it at all, thinks of it fondly as a boy's straggling
nosegay, somewhat wilted in a hot eager hand, clumsily
tied together with honest love.

EDWIN ARLINGTON ROBINSON

Born Head Tide, Maine, December 22, 1869.
Entered Harvard but remained only two years. Secured a position in the customs service through the influence of President Theodore Roosevelt, one of the first admirers of his verse. Won the Pulitzer Prize three times: 1922, 1925, and 1928. Author *The Town Down the River* (1910), *Merlin* (1917), *Tristram* (1927). *Collected Poems* were first issued in 1921. He made his home in New York, and summered at Peterboro, New Hampshire. He died in New York, April 6, 1935.

THE FIRST SEVEN YEARS appeared in Part Four of The Colophon; December, 1930.

The pencil draft of the manuscript that Mr. Robinson wrote for The Colophon practically answers all our questions. Furthermore, we have this comment from one of his literary executors.

Law Offices
M. S. & I. S. Isaacs
475 Fifth Avenue
New York
January 21, 1937

Dear Mr. Adler:

Replying to yours of the 19th, I think you may safely conclude that the pencil manuscript of Mr. Robinson's article is

[161]

B·C·D·F·G·H·I·J·K·L·M·N·E·A·R·O·P·Q·S·T·U·V·W·X·Y·Z

the original draft. Usually where there was a second draft, it would be on one side of the paper only, and in little larger handwriting; although I cannot be sure that this was his invariable practice.

Trusting that this fully answers your inquiries, I am
Faithfully yours,

Lewis M. Isaacs

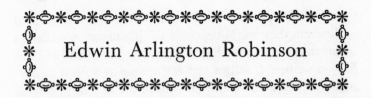
WHENEVER I have occasion to turn the leaves of a rather formidable looking book of mine entitled *Collected Poems*, the sight of a section of it called *The Children of the Night* is likely to make me realize unwillingly, and with an effort, that some of those early poems were written more than forty years ago. In those days time had no special significance for a certain juvenile and incorrigible fisher of words who thought nothing of fishing for two weeks to catch a stanza, or even a line, that he would not throw back into a squirming sea of language where there was every word but the one he wanted. There were strange and iridescent and impossible words that would seize the bait and swallow the hook and all but drag the excited angler in after them, but like that famous catch of Hiawatha's, they were generally not the fish he wanted. He wanted fish that were smooth and shining and subtle, and very much alive, and not too strange; and presently, after long patience and many rejections, they began to bite.

Many of those slippery victims went into the preparation and final accomplishment of innumerable short poems and sonnets that had certainly many faults and at least one merit. For me, at any rate, there was a sort of merit in their not being quite like anything else—or anything that I remembered. But a kindly providence had given me a modicum of common sense that was always reminding me of my age—from sixteen to twenty—and warning me that my somewhat peculiar productions, no matter how radical or different they might be, could not in the nature of things be much more than technical exercises. I had read of John Milton writing *L'Allegro* and *Il Penseroso* at a most annoyingly early age and could only make the best of it, having been told that the English mind matures anywhere from five to ten years earlier than our minds over here. That was a comfort, for I was compelled to acknowledge, and even to myself, that I could not write *L'Allegro* or *Il Penseroso*, no matter how hard I might try. It was a concession, but I made it.

It was about my seventeenth year when I became violently excited over the structure and music of English blank verse, and in order to find out a little more about it I made—of all things possible—a metrical translation of Cicero's first oration against Catiline, which we were reading in school. It began well enough, and with no difficulty:

> *O Catiline, how long will you abuse*
> *Our patience?*

That was easy, and invited me to go on. If it lacked something of the vindictive resonance that we feel in the Latin, the fault was not in me but in the English language, for which I was not responsible. So I went on with it until the whole diatribe, which is not short, lay before me in a clean copy of impeccable pentameters (I thought then that they were impeccable) which looked at a glance very much as an equal amount of *Paradise Lost* would have looked if I had copied it on the same quality of paper. It may not have been poetry, and probably wasn't, but many portions of it had music and rhythm and an unmistakable presence of what is nowadays called a punch—for which Cicero may possibly deserve some credit. It was written and rewritten with a prodigality of time that only youth can afford, with an elaborately calculated variation of the cæsura, and with a far more laborious devotion than was ever expended

B·C·D·F·G·H·I·J·K·L·M·N·E·A·R·O·P·Q·S·T·U·V·W·X·Y·Z

on anything that I was supposed to be studying. When this rather unusual bit of minstrelsy was accomplished, and followed by a similar treatment of long passages from Virgil, I had the profound and perilous satisfaction of knowing a great deal more about the articulation and anatomy of English blank verse than I had known before. A few years later I nearly wore myself out one summer over a metrical translation, made from a literal English version furnished by a schoolmate of mine who is now Professor Smith of Amherst College, of the *Antigone*—which has disappeared mysteriously, and I trust for ever. Not that it was altogether bad; it was just one of those juvenile experiments that we would rather not have brought in evidence against us. If ever it should come to light, I hope the finder will heed my solemn request that it shall not be published.

It must have been about the year 1889 when I realized finally, and not without a justifiable uncertainty as to how the thing was to be done, that I was doomed, or elected, or sentenced for life, to the writing of poetry. There was nothing else that interested me, and I was rational enough to keep the grisly secret to myself. Perhaps I was afraid of being arrested; perhaps I was afraid that my father and mother, the best and kindest of parents, would have had my head examined if they had known what was going on inside it. They knew already that I was unpractical, and indifferent—to say it mildly—to any of the world's reputable pursuits, and they knew that I was inordinately addicted to reading the somewhat unusual amount of poetry that was in the house; but they did not know the worst. My father died without suspecting it; my mother did not live to see printed evidence of it—which, while it would have interested her intensely, might still have given her reason to see more darkly than ever, in her affectionate imagination, a prospect that was dark enough even for me whenever I strained my mind's eye for the sight of more than a little of it at a time. For something told me at an early age, long before there was any material reason for worry, that they whose lives are to be chronically hazardous and uncertain should take only short views ahead. Before the family fortune, such as it was, went to smash, I could see it going and could see myself setting out alone on what was inevitably to be a long and foggy voyage. The prospect was interesting, if it was not altogether reassuring.

But I was not much occupied then with the future, which must somehow or other, so far as I was concerned, fulfill itself in its own. I was chiefly occupied with the composition of short poems and sonnets, which I would read to my old friend and neighbor, Dr. A. T. Schumann, who was himself a prolific writer of sonnets, ballades and rondeaus, and a master of poetic technique. As I shall never know the extent of my indebtedness to his interest and belief in my work, or to my unconscious absorption of his technical enthusiasm, I am glad for this obvious opportunity to acknowledge a debt that I cannot even estimate. Perhaps I was not quite veracious in saying a moment ago that my poetic aspirations and determinations were exclusively a matter of my own knowledge, for the doctor must have known, with his knowledge of humanity and human frailty, the dangerous fate that was before me. In fact, he told me once that I should have to write poetry or starve, and that I might do both—although he did not believe that I should starve, or not exactly. That was encouraging, and I have never forgotten it. If he had cared as much about "the numerous ills inwoven with our frame" as he did about the metrical defects and tonal shortcomings of the major and minor English poets, he would surely have been a most remarkable doctor; as it was, I am sure, that he was one of the most remarkable metrical technicians that ever lived, and an invaluable friend to me in those years of apprenticeship when time, as a commodity to be measured and respected, did not exist. There were such things as hours and days and weeks on clocks and calen-

E. A. Robinson

dars, but it made no difference to me how few or many of them went to my getting a few lines to go as I wanted them to go. It was no uncommon performance of mine to write a sonnet in twenty minutes or half an hour, and work over it for twenty days—an expenditure of life for which the doctor could not conscientiously reproach me. One afternoon I found him in his office fairly swelling with triumph and satisfaction, having straightened out a refractory line of his that had been bothering him for two years. All this may have been bad for the practice of medicine, but apparently it was a part of his fate, and of mine.

After two years at Harvard College (1891-1893) where I made several good friends, I returned to my home in Gardiner, Maine, and worked steadily at my unaccredited profession until 1897, when I went to New York. Sometimes I wondered what my friends and neighbors thought of me, but as it could make no manner of difference to me what they thought, there was nothing for me to do but to go on filing and fitting words until I had words enough to make a book. For three years I sent my wares incessantly to every reputable monthly and weekly periodical in the country—there were not so many in those days as there are now—and invariably got them back, or all but a few that were accepted by some of the less prominent publications or now and then by a newspaper. My collection of rejection slips must have been one of the largest and most comprehensive in literary history, with innumerable duplicates. One sonnet, "The Clerks," having gone the rounds with many others, was sent finally to the *New York Sun,* and was promptly returned with a piece of white paper on which was written with a blue pencil, "Unavailable. Paul Dana." I am surprised and puzzled to this day that Mr. Dana should have gone to that trouble when he might have had a neat pile of printed slips at his elbow. He may have used them all in returning other sonnets.

Whether or not it was the return of *The Clerks* from

the *Sun* that started and set going some new wheels in my emotional machinery is more than I can say at this time. But something set them going, and their persistence assured me at last that there would be no use or sense in any further attempt to make my work known to the public through the periodical press. I was not conscious of analyzing my feelings at the time, but a retrospective consideration of them compels me to suspect myself of being quietly and thoroughly disgusted. I hope it was not so bad as that, but probably it was. At any rate, I made a selection of about forty poems from everything that I had written during the past six or seven years and made a small book of them, reasoning prematurely and wildly that publishers might find something in them that editors had overlooked. But a few experimental attacks in their direction only brought the manuscript back to me with a speed that would be remarkable with even our present aerial facilities. There was something wrong somewhere, and as I was still confident that the poems had nothing worse than a new idiom to condemn them, the fault must be somewhere else. By degrees I began to realize that those well-typed and harmless looking verses of mine might as well be written, so far as possible attention or interest on the part of editors and publishers was concerned, in the language of the Senegambians.

> *I did not think that I should find them there*
> *When I came back again*

was evidently too much: and not only for Mr. Dana, but for the traditional sensibilities of editors in general.

There was nothing left, so far as I could see, but to print the unwelcome little volume at my own expense, and to let it find its way to recognition or to oblivion as it might. With an obstinate confidence that somehow strengthened itself with each new rebuff, I was unable to foresee oblivion for the poems, though I could foresee too surely a long and

[168]

obscure journey for them before they should have more than a small number of friends. Fortunately for me, a few really responsive and intelligent readers were all that I should expect or require for some years to come, but I wanted those few readers badly, and knew well enough that I was going to have them. So it was with no feeling of humiliation or surrender that I sent the manuscript to the Riverside Press, from which highly respectable establishment I received in due time three hundred copies of an inconspicuous blue-covered little pamphlet, which I had named, rather arbitrarily, from the first and the last poem: *The Torrent and The Night Before*. The entire edition cost me fifty-two dollars, which I am told is appreciably less than one pays today for a single copy. I am naturally a well-wishing person, and not in the least vindictive; yet sometimes I have wished that all surviving editors and publishers who pointed a cold nose at those early poems might find themselves afflicted with a collector's frenzy for the possession of a copy of that first book of mine published in 1896. My constructive imagination would be mean enough to enjoy the sight of them signing cheques for it.

When my three hundred copies arrived (or three hundred and twelve, to be exact) I knew that something important had happened to me. It never occurred to my confident enthusiasm that their arrival, or their existence, might not be important to anybody else, and it was therefore with an untroubled zeal that I began to send them out into the world—most of them to periodicals for possible critical notice, and to strangers who were known to me only by reputation. Perhaps thirty or forty of them went to friends and acquaintances, but the most of them went, as they were intended to go, unsolicited and unannounced into the unknown. Only a few of them—possibly ten or twelve—failed in drawing from its recipient some sort of response. Considering its unimpressive appearance as a publication and the complete obscurity of its origin, it was received generally with a respect and an enthusiasm that was gratifying, and was all that I needed to keep me going through the years of obscurity and material uncertainty that were so definitely before me. My incurable belief in what I was doing made me indifferent alike to hostility or neglect. There was far more neglect than hostility, as a matter of fact, although now and then a protesting voice would be heard saying something that was not especially complimentary or true. One critic took refuge in paraphrase, merely wishing in print that my poetry might be sent to the bourne from which no poetry returns.

I may say in conclusion, and in reply to several who have asked for information on the subject, that I have no means of knowing how many copies of *The Torrent* are now in existence. Considering the few that have come up for sale, perhaps it may be safe to assume that of the original three hundred, something like half that number may have been lost or destroyed. Thirty-four years may be considered a fairly long life for an obscure pamphlet, and especially for a pamphlet of unorthodox poetry by an unknown writer who could find no publisher for it but himself.

In 1897 most of these poems, along with a number of new ones, were published under the title of *The Children of the Night*.

CARL VAN VECHTEN

Born Cedar Rapids, Iowa, June 17, 1880.
Ph.B., University of Chicago, 1903. Was a musical or dramatic critic on various newspapers. Married to Fania Marinoff, the Russian actress. Author *Music and Bad Manners* (1916), *The Tiger in the House* (1920), *Peter Whiffle* (1922), *The Tattooed Countess* (1924). Home: New York.

N O T E S   F O R   A N   A U T O B I O G R A P H Y appeared in Part Three of The Colophon; June, 1930.

101 Central Park West
New York
Cable: Carl Vecht, New York
December 20, 1936

Dear Elmer, I make the first draft of anything I write, and succeeding drafts, on a typewriter with the very fingers with which I am writing this (and on the same typewriter). I have never employed a secretary; nor have I ever dictated any of my work. In preparing a book I usually make three complete drafts and any number of changes on each. I also usually receive three sets of proofs (galleys, page, and another set of page proofs after corrections have been made). I make many corrections and even fundamental alterations in the first two sets. I try to keep my fingers off the third for anything but typographical errors. I believe my bill

A·B·D·E·F·G·H·I·J·K·L·M·C·V·V·N·O·P·Q·R·S·T·U·W·X·Y·Z

for excess corrections in the typeset Nigger Heaven, for example, ran to something over $200.00. I never get through with a book and every time it is reprinted I make as many changes as time or circumstances permit.

Dear Elmer, I have been in bed for a week and am sitting up to write this. Furthermore, as you know, I moved this fall. Hence, I cannot honor your request for a sheet of typical manuscript at this moment. HOWEVER, if you can wait a few days, and WANT ONE VERY BADLY, let me know and I'll see what I can do.

Best Scotch grouse to you and four plovers' eggs,

!Carlo V.V.!

Carl Van Vechten

I CANNOT remember the time when I was not trying to write, often with no reasonable amount of skill. I think it would be true to say that I always wanted to write (although I also cherished other ambitions: at one period I craved a career as a concert pianist; at another, as a jockey) but I do not think at first it occurred to me that I wanted to write a book.

At the University of Chicago I contributed some really vile sketches to the *Weekly* and during the same period wrote a rather better letter or two for the *Pulse*, the monthly organ of the Cedar Rapids (Iowa) High School. Also at the University I specialized in English with Robert Morss Lovett, the best teacher I ever had and still my friend, William Vaughn Moody, and Robert Herrick. Herrick, I believe, was the first novelist I ever met and a hero to me for many years on this account.

My themes were pretty dreadful—I have retained some of them, probably the best: so I am not criticizing from memory—but my energy in creating them was enormous, and once or twice I almost hit on something. My modest design was to prepare myself for work on a newspaper. On leaving college, with a boost from Sam Paquin, a fraternity brother, I easily satisfied this intention, joining the forces of Hearst's *Chicago American*. As the staff of this paper at this epoch included such brilliant reporters as Hugh Fullerton, Charles Finnegan, and Charlie

Fitzmorris, the Chicago boy who beat Nelly Bly's record in a race around the world, and who afterwards became Chicago's Chief of Police, naturally I was offered but scant opportunity to write. I was sent out to gather information regarding "stories" which I telephoned in and the accounts that appeared in the paper were the work of these "rewrite" men. I was also deputed to fetch photographs of persons in the news and was so successful at this humble occupation that I was kept at it interminably, and only actually broke away from it, and the kindly tyranny of Moses Koenigsberg, the city editor, when I left for New York in 1906.

My first home in New York was a large room at 39 West Thirty-ninth Street where Sinclair Lewis occupied an adjoining chamber, but I cannot describe him as the second novelist I met because at that time he was yet to publish his first book. From the *Chicago American* I went to *The New York Times*, but previously I had sold a paper on Richard Strauss's *Salome*, produced during that winter at the Metropolitan Opera House, to the *Broadway Magazine*. It appeared in the January 1907 number of that periodical. Theodore Dreiser was the editor who ordered and accepted this paper. He was, I fancy, the second novelist I encountered. I saw him frequently at this period—six years after the publication of *Sister Carrie*—and we discussed the possibility of my writing further articles. One about Columbia University, I think, was ordered, and perhaps written, but certainly not published. On the staff of the magazine was a picturesque young man called Harris Merton Lyon, the "De Maupassant, Jr." of Dreiser's *Twelve Men*. Shortly after I sold my paper on *Salome* to Dreiser, I was engaged as assistant to Mr. Richard Aldrich on the music department of *The New York Times*. By this time I was thoroughly convinced that I wanted to be a music critic and write for the magazines. It was not long before I had satisfied both these ambitions. I also served for nearly a year as Paris cor-

[174]

respondent of *The New York Times*. It had not yet occurred
to me that I would write a book.

In September 1913, I joined the *New York Press*, as
dramatic critic. In June 1914, Mr. Frank Munsey, the eccentric owner of this newspaper, decided to dispense with
my services. A few months later he decided to dispense with
the paper itself. After a trip abroad and a short experience
as the editor of a dying magazine of parts which published
articles about Gertrude Stein and early poems by Wallace
Stevens, I recalled a remark which had been made to me
by Mr. George Moore, the third novelist I met. I had originally encountered Mr. Moore at Jacques Blanche's in
Paris and he had talked so well and I had remembered so
much of what he said that afterwards I had recorded the
conversation. When, later, I had shown him this paper, he
had demanded of me: "Why don't you make this the nu-
cleus for a book of essays?" Now, in the spring of 1915, with
no occupation, I began to consider Mr. Moore's casual
suggestion, also bearing in mind the sapient advice of Jack
Reed, who had read a good many of my articles: "Why
don't you try to write the way you talk?"

It happened, however, that aside from my paper on
Mr. Moore—which, by the way, has never yet appeared in
a book—I believed that my best writing dealt with music.
It was therefore seven musical articles that I chose to work
over to form the contents of my first book, *Music After the
Great War*. One of these, "Massenet and Women," had
been printed in the *New Music Review* as early as February
1913. After the book was typed it seemed reasonable to me
that a music publisher would be the most appropriate person with whom to place the manuscript of a book in music.
I had often encountered Mr. Rudolph Schirmer in the
Opera House and so it was to him that I handed the manuscript. He received it without cordiality, but, on the advice
of his reader, it was immediately accepted and was published in December of the same year: 1915. I was invited to

choose the format and I did so by making reasonable alter-
ations in the format of the American edition of Mr. Wells's
Boon. Among others, Mr. H. L. Mencken thought well of
Music After the Great War and said so at some length in the
Smart Set.

If my first book was published without difficulty, my
second book was rejected, and as a matter of fact it has
never been published to this day. It is the only book I have
ever written which has not been accepted for immediate
publication. Its title was *Pastiches et Pistaches*, a title I afterwards employed to head a series of random notes written
for the *Reviewer*. Among the thirteen publishers who rejected it was Alfred A. Knopf. Unlike the others, however,
Mr. Knopf was curious enough to read my first book and
interested enough in that to invite me to come to see him.
At that time, he occupied a single room, with a cubby-hole
for a boy, in an office building on Forty-second Street. He
resembled a Persian prince and certainly behaved like one.
His suggestion was that as I knew a good deal about music
and seemed to be able to write about it I should stick to
that general subject for the moment. The result of this conversation was the planning and execution of *Music and Bad
Manners*, immediately accepted and published by Mr.
Knopf, who has been my publisher ever since.

In the winter of 1920 I conceived the idea which led to
the composition of *Peter Whiffle*. When it was completed I
took the manuscript to Mr. Knopf. I had not told him that
I was writing a novel. As a matter of fact I do not believe
I knew that I was writing a novel. However, after it appeared, the reviewers began to declare that it was a novel
and so, to my astonishment, I found myself a novelist and
sat down to write, with the greatest ease, *The Blind Bow-
Boy*.

In this brief account of my adventures in the art of
writing, I have not spoken of my first appearance as a
player of chamber-music (witnesses still live who have

heard me perform the piano parts in violin and piano sonatas by Richard Strauss, César Franck, and Edvard Grieg) nor have I dwelt on my debuts as actor and composer, careers which I was not encouraged to follow.

HUGH WALPOLE

Born Auckland, New Zealand, March 13, 1884.
Educated at King's School, Canterbury, and Emmanuel
College, Cambridge, England. Served with the Russian
Red Cross in the World War, 1914–16. Tried preaching,
teaching, and book reviewing, in the order named. Author
The Duchess of Wrexe (1914), *Jeremy* (1919), *Harmer John*
(1926), *Rogue Herries* (1930). Home: London, England.

MY FIRST PUBLISHED BOOK appeared in Part
Two of The Colophon; April, 1930.

> *Brackenburn*
> *Manesty Park*
> *Keswick*
> *January 3, 1937*

Dear Mr. Adler:

> *I don't know whether these notes are any good.*
> *I write all my work by hand.*
> *It is typed away from home.*
> *I can't dictate except short articles, letters, etc.*
> *Generally two proofs are enough.*
> *I make many changes in type.*
> *I enclose a page of* MSS.

> > *Yours sincerely*
> > > *Hugh Walpole*

Hugh Walpole

INTO what distant ages do I look back and to what supreme and unjustified confidence! I gather, however, that this account is intended to be practical rather than sentimental. If I can I will recover the facts—but how difficult the facts are after all these years, and how shadowy their outlines!

Of one thing at least I can be sure. That I had been writing novels ever since I was six, and of another fact also —that I never had the slightest doubt but that one day I would be published. Now why I was so certain I can't conceive. No one else had the very slightest confidence in me. There was very little "writing" at that time in the family. Later on my father published works of theology, and very good some of them were, but my father never cared so very greatly for the arts. His impulse was quite another.

No one encouraged me to read, to care for pictures and music. I had no literary relations unless you can call a two-century uncle, Horace Walpole, or a fifty-year-distant uncle, Barham of the *Ingoldsby Legends*, relations. And yet I wrote as I breathed, in quite the old-fashioned way—as indeed I have done ever since.

My taste, from six to twenty, was for historical romances. I read them passionately and I wrote them passionately. I read Scott then for the story—the absence of which is, I understand, the reason why no one reads him today. And yet today no one cares for story. Why should he not be read then for character, his supreme claim? Perhaps soon again he will be. Shades also of Francis Marion Crawford and Stanley Weyman, let me pay you this transient tribute! What reassurance you gave to at least one unhappy and bewildered childhood! And even now I dare to assert that *Saracinesca* and *St. Ilario*, *The Castle Inn* and *Count Hannibal*, are beyond the present powers of any living novelist whether of England or America.

So, under every constant evidence of disapproval, I wrote my romances, wrote them, bound them in brown paper and put them away. I had then the true "writer's fervor." I didn't care whether anyone read them or no. I wrote only for my own delight.

Then, during my last year at school and my first year at Cambridge, I wrote a long modern story and called it *Troy Hanneton*. Only one living person ever saw it, Arthur Christopher Benson, a friend of my father's, a very loyal friend of my own. He read it (or part of it—it was in my own atrocious handwriting), wrote me a kind letter advising me to destroy it, urging me to read the works of George Moore, and finally with great kindness advising me to put novel-writing out of my head, as novelist I was not, nor ever would be!

Now here was an odd thing. I never in my life had such an incentive to continue novel-writing as from this letter of Benson's. I cannot explain it, but I knew after reading that letter of Benson's that I *was* a novelist and that nothing henceforward would stop me. It was not that I did not value Benson's opinion (I at once followed his advice and burnt *Troy Hanneton*), but his reasons against my being a novelist seemed to me all the wrong ones. I still think they were.

I began at once another novel entitled *The Abbey*. At this I strove for a year. It was my first attempt at a full-grown novel—not, as *Troy* was, rather plaintive autobiography.

As soon as he set your

out of doors he felt as

happily

...gh their families wheel...

greet him with a glad welcome.

This was an egotism

...me.

generally to be reprehended

consider

...those who ~~take~~ as ... ...

gentlemen seriously. but for

those who do not know ...

much to be said for

any sort of gladness which

By the end of a year I was in so desperate a confusion, so many characters were driving aimlessly in so many different directions, that I had to abandon it, but it has this interest for me, that the ten odd chapters of it held the germ of a book published nearly twenty years later, *The Cathedral*.

I abandoned it and began another—*The Wooden Horse*. I was at this time for my sins a schoolmaster, and when I had written the first half of the book I showed it to a fellow schoolmaster, a man much older than myself, of whose abilities I had the greatest opinion. He read it and returned it to me, saying sorrowfully that whatever else I might be I was not a novelist.

This again did not in the slightest deter me. I finished the thing, abandoned schoolmastering and came up to London with thirty pounds in all the world and not the least prospect of a job anywhere.

Indeed I have reason now, with my fuller knowledge, to marvel at my hardihood. I did not, I must honestly admit, think that *The Wooden Horse* was a masterpiece. I suffered then, as I still suffer, from the shabby fashion in which characters who have been living with you in close intimacy for years vanish into air as soon as the word "Finis" is written on the final page.

It is my longing to recover some of their company. I suppose that has led me so often to drag characters by the hair of their heads from one book into another—a most reprehensible proceeding, but one that will, I suppose, carry on to the last. They were alive once—why should they not be alive again? And, sometimes, they do return.

I had no illusions about *The Wooden Horse*. I have, I think, never had any illusions about any book of mine. Only after a great distance of time do you recover an affection for them. I knew that this book had no importance, but I also knew that between *The Abbey* and this I had in some mysterious way stepped from the amateur to the young professional. Too much the professional. I fancy that only now, twenty years after, I am recovering some of the amateur again, but that too may be illusion.

In any case I had a friend and I sent him my book. This friend is the only man, as I think, who has ever written about Cornwall as a poet should. Charles Marriott is his name; he was once a novelist, is now art critic for the London *Times*. His novels—*The Column, Genevra, The Catfish* and others will be rediscovered one day. His prose cannot be lost: he writes about Cornwall like an inspired angel. In any case his was the first encouragement I ever received, and I'll never forget my debt. He said kind things, wise things, cautionary things. I showed it also, I remember, to E. M. Forster, whom I had met in Germany. He was then at the beginning of his grand career, and he is as modest and gentle now as he was modest and gentle then. He can't have liked *The Wooden Horse* very much, I imagine, but he said what he could. At any rate he read it and said that it should be published.

I can see him now, long, shambling and shy, looking beyond me into some space of his own (and he has always occupied a room entirely of his own; he has another room for visitors and he very often isn't there when they think that he is), trying to tell me some of the things that my book ought to have. He couldn't, of course; no one ever can. But I was grateful, and he was, I am sure, intensely glad when the little matter was closed.

But, thus encouraged, I had no hesitation now in approaching a publisher. I would, I thought, begin at the top and work my way down the list. The top for me at that time was the publisher of Thackeray and the Brontës, the firm of Smith Elder, now defunct. The original Mr. Smith was one of my heroes, for had he not been kind to Charlotte and soothed the nerves of William Makepeace? So I scraped my shillings together, *The Wooden Horse* was typed, done up in brown paper, fastened with pink string (I remember very clearly how my Chelsea landlady, Mrs. King, a little woman with long legs like a sparrow on stilts, did this part of the job for me) and sent it off.

I sat down then and waited. I had managed, with my usual luck, to receive some reviewing on the *Standard* newspaper, and for this I received three pounds a week. I was then perfectly happy in my two basement rooms in Glebe Place, Chelsea—I have never been happier. I sat down and waited. In spite of my confidence I was assured that I would be rejected. It couldn't conceivably be that my book would be published by the publisher of Thackeray and the Brontës!

I returned one evening to my Chelsea basement. A letter. An acceptance from Mr. Smith. It is true that he did not offer me any money, but then he did not wish *me* to pay any money either.

It is a platitude that never again can one know such joy as that first acceptance brings. I have known different joys since then—greater ones perhaps. But the exact taste and flavor of that first one has never been repeated. I rushed from my basement down to the river, where was a small inn known as the Good Intent. This was inhabited by artists of a sort; they sat all together in solemn assembly at one large table. I had never before dared to mingle with them. Now I rushed into their midst, told them my news, demanded that my health should be drunk. They drank it. Some of them are friends of mine yet, although the Good Intent, with Smith Elder and the *Standard*, is no more.

That young man who flourished *The Wooden Horse* in those artistic faces is, contrary to general information, still here.

EDITH WHARTON

Born New York, January 24, 1862.
Educated at home. Widow. Honorary Litt.D., Yale.
Officer Legion of Honor of France and Chevalier Order of
Leopold of Belgium. Won Pulitzer Prize in 1920 with her
novel, *The Age of Innocence*. In 1924 was awarded the gold
medal of the National Institute of Arts and Letters. Author
Ethan Frome (1911), *The Custom of the Country* (1913), *A Son
at the Front* (1923). Home: Pavillon Colombe, Saint-Brice
sous-Forêt (Seine et Oise), France.

THE WRITING OF ETHAN FROME appeared
in Part Eleven of The Colophon; September, 1932.

> Sainte-Claire le Château
> Hyères (Var)
> 26 January 1937

Dear Sir:

*Mrs. Wharton asks me, in reply to your request, to en-
close a page of manuscript which will give your readers an idea
of the way in which she works.*

*Will you kindly return the manuscript to the above ad-
dress when you have finished with it?*

> *Yours very truly*
> Mrs. J. Fridérich
> *Secretary*

[187]

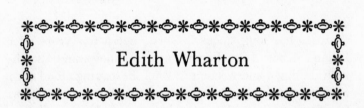

Edith Wharton

THE CONDITIONS in which *Ethan Frome* originated
have remained much more clearly fixed in my memory
than those connected with any of my other stories, owing
to the odd accident of the tale's having been begun in
French. Early in the nineteen hundreds I happened to be
spending a whole winter in Paris, and it occurred to me
to make use of the opportunity to polish and extend my
conversational French; for though I had spoken the language since the age of four I had never had occasion to
practise it for any length of time, at least with cultivated
people, having frequently wandered through France as a
tourist, but never lived there for more than a few weeks
consecutively. Accordingly, it was arranged that I should
read and talk for so many hours a week with a young
French professor; and soon after our studies began he suggested that before each of his visits I should prepare an
"exercise" for him.

I have never been able, without much mental anguish,
to write anything but a letter or a story, and as stories come
to me much more easily than letters, I timidly asked him if
a story would "do," and, though obviously somewhat surprised at the unexpected suggestion, he acquiesced with
equal timidity. Thus the French version of *Ethan Frome*
began, and ploughed its heavy course through a copy-book
or two; then the lessons were interrupted and the Gallic
"Ethan" abandoned, I forget at what point in his career.

The copy-book containing this earliest version of his adventures has long since vanished; but a few years later Ethan's history stirred again in my memory, and I forthwith sat down and wrote it in English, reading aloud each evening what I had done during the day to a friend as familiar as I was with the lonely lives in half-deserted New England villages, before the coming of the motor and the telephone. The legend that Henry James suggested my transposing the French "composition" into an English tale —a fable I have frequently come across of recent years— must be classed among the other inventions which honour me by connecting my name with his in the field of letters. I am not sure if he even saw the French beginning of the tale, but he certainly did not suggest its rewriting in English, and never read the story, or heard of it again, till it appeared in print in the latter language.

While I am on the subject of literary fables, I might as well destroy another which likewise concerns *Ethan Frome*. Not long since I read a thoughtful article on the making of fiction, in which the author advanced the theory that in a given case a certain perspective might be necessary to the novelist, and that one might conceivably write a better book about Main Street if one lived as far away from it as Paris or Palermo; in proof of which *Ethan Frome* was cited as an instance of a successful New England story written by some one who knew nothing of New England. I have no desire to contest the theory, with which, in a certain measure, I am disposed to agree; but the fact is that *Ethan Frome* was written after a ten years' residence in the New England hill country where Ethan's tragedy was enacted, and that during those years I had become very familiar with the aspect, the dialect and the general mental attitude of the Ethans, Zeenas and Mattie Silvers of the neighbouring villages. My other short novel of New England life, *Summer*, which deals with the same type of people involved in a

have failed to ~~seize~~ ~~upon~~ the mysterious quality
which seems, above all others, to have the
antiseptic quality of keeping a novel alive. One
reader may wish to prove ~~clay~~ to be one thing,
another reader another; "style," "that undefinable"
yet so plentifully defined attitude, it
perhaps mat- ~~style~~ ~~can~~ ~~corrupts~~ ~~interfaces~~ ~~in the~~
style can, in fact, evaluate a tale — that
is ~~sure~~ ~~to its~~ Environments & semblance of
vitality. But ~~style~~ ~~can~~ ~~in a great~~ ~~the~~
~~in a tale~~ ~~can~~ ~~the~~ ~~characters'~~
lifelikeness behind-behind feeling & air ~~air~~
In examining the question, one is confronted
sooner or later by ~~necessary~~ ~~the~~ ~~question~~

A·B·C·D·F·G·H·I·J·K·L·M·E·W·N·O·P·Q·R·S·T·U·V·X·Y·Z

different tragedy of isolation, might, one would suppose, have helped to prove to the legend-makers that I knew something at first hand of the life and the people into whose intimacy I had asked my readers to enter with me on two successive occasions.

INDEX

Adams, John Wolcott, 27
Adler, Elmer, viii
Alden, Henry Mills, 69
Aldrich, Thomas Bailey, 52
Aldrich, Richard, 174
Anderson, Sherwood, 3–7
Armstrong, Martin, 64

Babb, James T., 127
Balzac, Honoré de, 56
Bara, Theda, 97
Barham, Richard Harris, 181
Baudelaire, Charles, 88
Beacon, Judge Madison W., 49–50
Beek, James, 143–145
Benchley, Robert C., 9–17
Benét, Stephen Vincent, 19–28
Benét, William Rose, 122
Bennett, Arnold, 119
Benson, Arthur Christopher, 182
Blackwell, Basil, 155, 156, 159
Blackwell, Sr., 152–153, 155–156
Blanche, Jacques, 175
Bly, Nellie, 174
Boyle, Peter G., 89–90
Bridgman, Donald, 27

Brontës, the, 184, 185
Browning, Robert, 27
Buck, Pearl, 29–34
Butler, Samuel, 59

Cabell, James Branch, 35–43
Cable, George W., 51
Caine, Hall, 132, 134
Canby, Henry Seidel, 154
Catilina, Lucius Sergius, 164
Chappell, George, 112–114, 116
Chesnutt, Charles Waddell, 47–56
Chesnutt, Helen M., 48
Chopin, Frédéric François, 78
Cicero, Marcus Tullius, 164
Cleveland, Grover, 101
Cody, William (Buffalo Bill), 15, 60
Cook, Grace Macgowan, 122
Coppard, A. E., 57–65
Corelli, Marie, 132, 134
Cowley, Abraham, 157
Crane, Stephen, 22
Crawford, Francis Marion, 182
Crawford, Jack, 158
Crowninshield, Frank, 113–115

Cunningham, Colonel A. B., 142

Curtis, Cyrus, 5

Curtis, Laura, 81

Dana, Paul, 167, 168

Deutsch, Babette, 90

Dickens, Charles, 56, 60

Dixon, Thomas, 51

Dobson, Austin, 157

Dobson, Zuleika, 152

d'Orleans, Charles, 155

Dostoevski, Feodor Michaelovitch, 56

Doubleday, Mrs. Frank, 70

Drake, James F., 157

Dreiser, Theodore, 67–71, 174

Dumas, Alexandre, 53, 54, 56

Dumas, Alexandre (Dumas *fils*), 53

Dunbar, Paul Laurence, 51

Dwiggins, W. A., 35

Early, Jubal, 81

Earp, T. W., 62

Eliot, T. S., 62

Elmore, James B., 21

Emmett, Burton, 156

Fairbanks, Douglas, 97

Ferrero, 26

Finnegan, Charles, 173

Fisher, Herbert, 157

Fitzmorris, Charlie, 173–174

Florey, Lou, 117

Forster, E. M., 184

Franck, César, 177

Fridérich, J., 187

Fullerton, Hugh, 173

Garrison, Francis J., 51, 53

Garrison, William Lloyd, 51

Golding, Louis, 64

Gordon, Charles S., 143–144

Grant, General Ulysses S., 78

Greeley, Horace, 82

Greenslet, Ferris, 80

Grieg, Edvard, 177

Guedalla, Philip, 153, 155

Halleck, General Henry Wager, 81

Hamilton, Lady Emma, 77

Hardy, Thomas, 62

Harris, Frank, 77

Harrison, Austin, 62, 63

Hart, William S., 97

Harte, Bret, 60

Heinemann, William, 70, 71

Hemingway, Ernest, 13–15, 17

Hemphill, Dorothy, 73

Herbert, A. P., 153, 155

Hergesheimer, Joseph, 73–83

Herrick, Robert, 173

Hogarth, William, Jr. (see Kent, Rockwell)

Hope, Anthony, 132

Howells, William Dean, 52, 53, 119

Isaacs, Lewis M., 161–162

Jackson, Andrew, 78

Jackson, Rachel, 78

James, Henry, 190

Janvier, Meredith, 145

Jeffers, Robinson, 85–91

Kantor, MacKinlay, 93–104

Keats, John, 151

Kennerley, Mitchell, 154

Kent, Rockwell, 105–116

Kipling, Rudyard, vii, 142

Kirstein, Lincoln, viii

Knox, Jack, 111
Knopf, Alfred A., 176
Koenigsberg, Moses, 174

Lal, Chaman, 60
Lane, John, 71
Lawrence, D. H., 77
Le Gallienne, Richard, 152, 159
Lewis, Sinclair, 117–123, 174
Lincoln, President Abraham, 80, 81–82
Lindsay, Vachel, 154
Lloyd, David, 32–33
London, Jack, 60
Lovett, Robert Morss, 173
Lyon, Harris Merton, 174

MacVeagh, Lincoln, 15
McArthur, James, 54
McFee, William, 125–138
McKee, Thomas, 70
Maisel, Max, 152
Marinoff, Fania, 171
Marriott, Charles, 184
Masefield, John, 26, 61, 154
Mencken, H. L., 139–146, 176
Mendoza, Ike, 151, 152
Mifflin, George H., 51, 53
Millay, Edna St. Vincent, 154
Miller, Francis Trevelyan, 102
Milne, A. A., 121
Milton, John, 164
Montez, Lola, 77
Moody, William Vaughn, 173
Moore, George, 88, 175, 182
Morley, Christopher, 147–159
Moult, Thomas, 64
Munsey, Frank, 175

Newton, A. Edward, 157
Norris, Frank, 69, 70

Olliver, Thomas, 61

Page, Thomas Nelson, 51
Page, Walter Hines, 52–53, 54
Paquin, Samuel, 173
Parker, Dorothy, 16
Pater, Walter, 132, 157
Perry, Bliss, 52
Perry, Susan U., 47
Pushkin, Alexander Sergivich, 53

Reed, John, 175
Richardson, Samuel, 56
Robey, George, 62
Robinson, Edwin Arlington, 22, 161–170
Roosevelt, President Theodore, 161
Rorty, James, 90

Sand, George, 78
Schirmer, Rudolph, 175
Schumann, Dr. A. T., 166–167
Scott, Sir Walter, 181–182
Seward, William Henry, Secretary of State, 80, 82
Shakespeare, William, 43, 60
Shay, Frank, 157
Sheridan, General Philip H., 78–83
Sherman, Frank Dempster, 157
Sherry, Louis, 114
Siegal, John, 142–144
Spingarn, Colonel Joel, 50
Squire, J. C., 62
Squires, Fred, 108–112
Starrett, Vincent, 141
Steig, William, 9
Stein, Gertrude, 175
Sterling, George, 90–91

Stevens, Wallace, 175
Stevenson, Robert Louis, 155
Stewart, Donald Ogden, 16
Stowe, Harriet Beecher, 51
Strauss, Richard, 174, 176

Taggard, Genevieve, 90
Taylor, Harold, 64–65
Thackeray, William Make-peace, 134, 184, 185
Thomas, Major-General George H., 102
Thompson, Francis, 22
Thurston, Katherine Cecil, 121
Tolstoi, Count Leo, 152
Tourgee, Judge Albion W., 51
Trelawny, Edward John, 44

Van Doren, Mark, 90–91, 154

Van Vechten, Carl, 55, 171–177
Vedder, Elihu, 28
Virgil (Publius Vergilius Maro), 165
Vorse, Mary Heaton, 123

Wagner, Richard, 78
Walpole, Horace, 119, 181
Walpole, Hugh, 119, 179–185
Walsh, Richard, 33
Wells, H. G., 22, 60, 119, 176
Weyman, Stanley, 182
Wharton, Edith, viii, 187–191
Wheatley, Phillis, 51
Whitman, Walt, 119, 152
Wilson, President Woodrow, 52
Winterich, John T., viii

Zangwill, Israel, 121